The Standard & Poor's Guide to the Perfect Portfolio

Five Steps to Allocate Your Assets and Ensure a Lifetime of Wealth

---

Michael Kaye

New York   Chicago   San Francisco   Lisbon   London   Madrid   Mexico City
Milan   New Delhi   San Juan   Seoul   Singapore   Sydney   Toronto

1 2 3 4 5 6 7 8 9 0 DOC/DOC 0 9 8 7

ISBN-13: 978-0-07-147934-9
ISBN-10: 0-07-147934-1

This publication is designed to provide accurate and authoritative information in regard to the subject matter covered. It is sold with the understanding that the publisher is not engaged in rendering legal, accounting, or other professional service. If legal advice or other expert assistance is required, the services of a competent professional person should be sought.

—*From a Declaration of Principles Jointly Adopted by a Committee of the American Bar Association and a Committee of Publishers and Associations*

McGraw-Hill books are available at special discounts to use as premiums and sales promotions, or for use in corporate training programs. For more information, please write to the Director of Special Sales, Professional Publishing, McGraw-Hill, Two Penn Plaza, New York, NY 10121-2298. Or contact your local bookstore.

This book is printed on acid-free paper.

To my father, Stan,
for all his love and support throughout my life

ACKNOWLEDGMENTS

There are a number of people who made this book a reality. I would like to thank George Gulla for accepting my idea for a book about creating a perfect portfolio. I would like to acknowledge Jim Dunn for giving me many ideas on ways to improve the book. Jim is a former treasurer of GTE and is presently a consultant for Standard & Poor's. I would also like to thank Leah Spiro for her editing. Going through my manuscript and fixing the grammatical mistakes was a monumental task.

I am very fortunate to have a very supportive family. I would like to thank my brother, Jon, for always being one of my biggest fans. Lastly, I would like to thank my wife, Emily, and my children, Megan and Shawn, for giving me a ton of encouragement while I was working on the book. Emily has been a wonderful wife, friend, and mother to our children. I would like to thank Megan and Shawn for always putting a smile on my face. They served as all the motivation I needed in tackling the task of writing this book. Every day, they prove to me, that even though I work on Wall Street and write about investments, there are much more important things in life than money.

CONTENTS

Introduction   1

PART I OVERVIEW

CHAPTER 1 ALLOCATING YOUR ASSETS:
THE FIVE MOST IMPORTANT STEPS   9

CHAPTER 2 ASSET ALLOCATION INGREDIENTS:
CHOOSING BETWEEN
THE ASSET CLASSES   29

CHAPTER 3 THE PACKAGING OF THE ASSET CLASS:
CHOOSING BETWEEN
A MUTUAL FUND
OR ANOTHER PACKAGED PRODUCT   51

CHAPTER 4 THE LOCATION OF YOUR ASSETS:
CHOOSING THE
RIGHT ACCOUNTS   69

CHAPTER 5 THE COST OF FINANCIAL ASSETS:
UNDERSTANDING THE IMPACT
OF FEES AND TAXES   91

CHAPTER 6   THE IMPACT OF ECONOMIC EVENTS
ON YOUR PORTFOLIO   105

PART II   **DETERMINING YOUR ASSET ALLOCATION MIX**

CHAPTER 7   THE THREE PRIMARY FACTORS IN
DETERMINING AN ALLOCATION MIX:
YOUR STAGE IN LIFE, WHEN YOU WILL NEED
THE MONEY, AND YOUR RISK TOLERANCE   115

CHAPTER 8   THE SIX SECONDARY FACTORS THAT
INFLUENCE HOW YOU CONSTRUCT
YOUR PORTFOLIO:
YOUR AGE, GENDER, MARITAL STATUS,
INVESTING EXPERIENCE, DEPENDENTS,
AND AFFLUENCE   135

PART III   **THE FIVE INVESTMENT STRATEGIES**

CHAPTER 9   CAPITAL PRESERVATION   147

CHAPTER 10   CONSERVATIVE INCOME   157

CHAPTER 11   GROWTH AND INCOME   171

CHAPTER 12   GROWTH   179

CHAPTER 13   AGGRESSIVE GROWTH   191

PART IV SUMMING IT UP

CHAPTER 14 TEN WAYS TO GROW AND
ENSURE WEALTH   201

CHAPTER 15 PUTTING IT ALL TOGETHER   211

Index   219

INTRODUCTION

The idea for this text came from reader feedback of my book *Standard & Poor's Guide to Selecting Stocks—Finding the Winners and Weeding Out the Losers*. Many readers told me that it was great to learn how to rank stocks, bonds, and mutual funds on the basis of their characteristics. For most of them the first major hurdle they faced as investors was deciding what percentage of stocks, bonds, and cash they should have in their portfolio. Many readers felt that being in the right asset classes at the right time would have a greater impact on their portfolios and their peace of mind than being in the right securities within these asset classes. Determining whether to purchase shares of Microsoft versus Pfizer was important but not nearly as important as deciding whether they should have 75% of their portfolio in stocks or only 25%. As the truism goes, "You cannot learn to run unless you know how to walk first."

Considerable academic research shows that the biggest factor in how your portfolio performs is how you allocate your assets. A famous 1986 study by Gary Brinson, L. Randolph Hood, and Gilbert Beebower concluded that asset allocation decisions explained more than 90% of the returns of the pension funds they studied. Mr. Brinson and his colleagues asserted that, on average, a portfolio's static target allocation explained most of its return and volatility over time, while security selection and market timing played only minor roles. Brinson and his colleagues found that pension funds were exposed to a high level of systematic market risk resulting in a high correlation between the funds actual returns and the returns of their benchmarks over time. In 2000, Roger Ibbotson and Paul Kaplan reported similar results using balanced mutual funds, and in 2003, the Vanguard Group also reported similar results. There has been some debate about how much asset allocation affects returns, but there can be no debate that asset allocation plays a major role in contributing to portfolio performance.

When deciding on investments, most people devote most of their time figuring out what stock to buy: stock X or stock Y. But the more important decision, which is often given little thought, is determining whether you should be in stocks or bonds at all and what percentage you should allocate toward each. Buying the right investment at the perfect time, which results in a doubling of its value, will not do much for your financial position if only 1% of your capital is in that asset.

If you had simply held a portfolio composed of a quarter each of the index funds of large U.S. stocks, small U.S. stocks, foreign stocks, and high-quality U.S. bonds over the past 10 or 20 years, you would have beaten over 90% of all professional money managers. The kicker is that you would have done it with considerably less risk. The truth is that over the long term, almost any reasonably balanced strategy using index funds will outperform the overwhelming majority of professional money managers. You will not see this fact advertised by many money management firms.

Today you are fortunate because efficient asset allocation is more attainable than at any other time in history. Proper asset allocation allows you the possibility of earning strong returns with reduced risk. In the current investment environment, it is very easy to get broad exposure to different investment classes with a single investment product at a very low cost. There are numerous mutual funds, both active and passive, and exchange-traded funds (ETFs) that can give you market-like returns in the equity, fixed income, and the short term cash markets in a diversified portfolio.

You have three main choices of instruments—mutual funds, exchange-traded funds, and individual securities. Broad indexes such as the S&P 500, Russell 2000, and the Lehman Aggregate can be purchased as mutual funds or ETFs. If you want to put your money in specific stocks and bonds, brokerage commissions are at the lowest levels they have ever been. Balanced mutual funds are available that combine different asset classes in a single portfolio. Asset allocation funds that have different asset classes in one portfolio and strategically adjust the weightings as a target date approaches are also available. These types of funds save you the time and effort of rebalancing the asset classes in your portfolio by yourself. The fund does it automatically for you.

Most brokerage firms have a published target allocation for a "typical" client. Unfortunately, no uniform asset allocation is right for every individual. Numerous personal circumstances can cause two seemingly similar people to require very different portfolios. Also the following broad trends that have emerged in society will have an impact on the way individuals manage their assets for years to come:

- People are living longer.
- People are entering and leaving the workforce at older ages.
- College costs are astronomical and outpace inflation year after year.
- More and more families have two wage earners.
- People are likely to switch jobs several times throughout their lifetimes.
- Health care costs keep rising.
- More marriages are ending in divorce.
- Credit is being used and misused more often.

Complicating these trends is the shift in most companies from defined benefit to defined contribution plans for managing employees' retirement income. Thus the onus falls on employees to decide how their assets are allocated and managed. The traditional pension where a longtime employee of a company could expect a certain annual payout in retirement is being phased out.

Furthermore, there is also no guarantee that the safety net of Social Security will be available for young people entering the workforce to help supplement their retirement income. Beginning in 2018, Social Security expenditures are expected to surpass payroll tax receipts. Already the age at which an individual can begin to receive full Social Security benefits has been raised from 65 to 67. The proportion of current workers to retirees will continue to decline as the baby boomers enter their retirement years. The first of the roughly 77 million baby boomers turned 60 in 2006. By the year 2030, approximately 20% of the population will be age 65 or older.

Despite having more responsibility for their future financial well-being, the amount of investment knowledge people have is dismally inadequate. The lack of financial literacy is frightening. Most people have not been taught how to manage money, and they are not willing to take the time necessary to do a good job managing their assets. Consider the following:

- Most people think that if they buy a mutual fund through a bank, the mutual fund is FDIC insured.
- 43% of American families spend more than they earn each year.

- Per household credit card debt averages more than $9,000.
- 23% of Americans save nothing on a monthly basis for retirement or a child's education.
- In 2003, more women filed for bankruptcy than graduated from college.

Asset allocation is a crucial tool that you should understand and use effectively to get your financial house in order. Most asset allocation studies have determined that peoples' age should be the primary component in deciding how to divide their money. A common theme is that younger people should be more aggressive by putting a high percentage of their assets in the stock market, while older folks should be more defensive and have their assets in highly rated bonds and short term money market instruments. The thinking goes that young people can ride out the inevitable ups and downs in the stock market because they have time on their side. Despite the volatility, over time, it is believed that stocks outperform all other asset classes. However, it is not prudent in any situation to have 100% of your entire portfolio in equities. The stock market crashes of 1929, 1987, and the sharp declines between 2000 and 2002 are testament to this wisdom.

Older people are usually told they need a safe, reliable stream of income because most are not drawing a paycheck from a job. The most common advice stresses safety and retention of capital. Although allocating 100% of an elderly person's portfolio in money market funds and low risk bonds may be safe, such a conservative portfolio may not be wise.

In one popular asset allocation approach, the percentage of equities you should hold is determined by subtracting your age from 100. According to this simplistic method, if you are 40 years old, you should have 60% of your portfolio in stocks.

While age is an important component, there are multiple factors that should be considered in determining your asset mix: your attitude toward risk, your return expectations, job status, income, tax situation, health, family status, and looming financial commitments are among a host of variables that need to be considered. It is imperative that you weigh your most important factors in determining how your money is to be divided. Individual circumstances are unique and can change suddenly, often without warning. Ultimately, individual investors require individual solutions. The perfect portfolio for you is not going to be the same as the perfect portfolio for your neighbor.

Three factors that I believe should be stressed in setting up your asset allocation are your risk tolerance, your looming financial obligations, and your stage of life. You have to feel comfortable with how your money is being managed. You should not have large positions of speculative stocks and junk bonds in your portfolio if you are extremely conservative and will be worried by any kind of loss. In planning your portfolio it is also imperative that you have a good idea of when you are going to need large specific outlays and approximately how much you will need. By knowing your attitude toward risk and when you will need a specific amount of money, you are more likely to develop a suitable investment plan and in the end be satisfied with the way your money is deployed. Lastly, the life stage that you are in rather than your age is important in determining how you divide up your assets. All things being equal, someone starting off in his or her career should have a different investment mix from someone who is about to retire.

From children receiving money from their grandparent to octogenarians on a fixed income, everyone can benefit from prudent asset allocation. Asset allocation done correctly can help investors achieve the Holy Grail in money management—high relative returns with low relative risk. This book is appropriate for readers looking to improve the way their portfolios are constructed. It deals with the subject of *asset allocation*, which is often overlooked despite the large impact it has on your investment results. I have tried my best to explain the concepts in plain English without the use of complex financial jargon. All the major investment products used in portfolio management will be discussed. Also the book will describe the ways in which people can adjust their assets as their personal circumstances change. Investment consultants and financial planners will be able to incorporate many of the ideas presented in helping them manage their clients' accounts.

Part 1 discusses what exactly asset allocation is and describes the characteristics of the investment products that are used to implement it. Parts 2 and 3 offer numerous model portfolio mixes based on risk profiles and investment goals that many people will be in at some point in their lives. Part 4 describes ways in which individuals can help protect their families and increase their wealth. The overall goal of the book is to provide you with a range of thoughtful, relevant, and reliable information that you can use to determine the appropriate course for your financial future.

Many people devote more time deciding what to do on a Friday night than they devote to planning their asset allocation and the security selection of their investments. Putting together an appropriate investment portfolio is not brain surgery. Anyone can learn how to allocate their assests. The knowledge gained can be applied throughout your lifetime and passed down to the next generation. All you need is the desire to learn about investments and a little bit of time. The potential payoff is well worth the investment.

It's never too late to get started. It's also never too late to give your existing portfolio a makeover. Asset allocation is not a one-time event; it's a lifelong process that requires fine-tuning. After all, your money is too important to invest without a plan. If you have any comments or questions about the material presented in the book, feel free to e-mail me at michael_kaye@sandp.com.

PART I

OVERVIEW

CHAPTER 1

ALLOCATING YOUR ASSETS

THE FIVE MOST IMPORTANT STEPS

It's not what we don't know that hurts us; it's what we know for sure that just ain't so.

MARK TWAIN

A sset allocation is a valuable tool that investors can use to answer questions such as:

- How do I avoid outliving my money?
- How should I invest my 401(k) plan?
- How much should I keep in an emergency fund and what asset class should it be in?
- I just inherited some money; now what should I do?
- How do I avoid giving the government more of my hard-earned money in the form of taxes and legally keep more for myself?
- Which are more suitable for me, mutual funds or exchange-traded funds?
- Should I take Social Security when I first become eligible or wait a few years?
- Which should I devote more savings to, future tuition bills or my retirement fund?

The answers to these questions all seem to include a "depends on" or "usually" modifier. I will discuss these questions and others, but I do want to stress that there is no one-size-fits-all solution to these questions. Many personal circumstances will have to be considered before coming up with answers.

Asset allocation is the process of determining the optimal way to divide a broad range of categories of assets (stocks, bonds, cash, and others) in a way that suits your investment time horizon and risk tolerance. It is an overriding strategy that can create a roadmap for building and managing your investment portfolio. This dynamic tool can efficiently handle both the changing economic environment as well as your ever-changing needs and goals as an investor. Studies have shown that your asset allocation decisions can explain over 90% of the total return of your portfolio. How you construct and divide your assets can be the difference between being able to retire comfortably at 60 or to not being able to afford to ever retire.

How different combinations of stocks and bonds performed between 1960 and 2005 is shown in Figure 1.1. (Stock market returns are based on the Standard & Poor's 500 Index from 1960 to 1970, the Dow Jones Wilshire 5000 Composite Index from 1971 through April 22, 2005, and the Morgan Stanley Capital International U.S. Broad Market Index after April 22, 2005. Bond market returns are based on the Standard & Poor's High Grade Corporate Index from 1960 to 1968, the Citigroup High Grade Index from 1969 to 1972, and the Lehman Brothers U.S. Government/Credit Bond Index from 1973 to 2005. The returns shown include the reinvestment of income, dividends, and capital gains distributions; they do not reflect the effects of investment expenses and taxes. Past performance is not a guarantee of future results. The real average annual return incorporates the impact of inflation). As you can see, the amount allocated to stocks and to bonds would have been a main determinant of the investor's financial well-being.

In my opinion, an investment plan that doesn't incorporate asset allocation is doomed to failure. Not using asset allocation is analogous to not asking for directions or not using a map when you are driving to a strange place. You will more than likely get lost and you will regret that you didn't ask for guidance or come prepared. Why take unnecessary chances with your money when you do not have to?

Asset allocation has a major impact on whether or not you meet your financial goals. If you do not take enough risks with your portfolio, your investments may not earn a large enough return to meet your goals. On the other hand, if you take too much risk, you may find your portfolio plummeting in value, making it difficult to meet your objectives. It is a

Figure 1.1 Performance of Stocks and Bonds from 1960 to 2005

Allocation Stocks %	Allocation Bonds %	Average Annual Return %	Real Average Annual Return %	Worst Annual Loss %	Number of Years with a Loss
0	100	7.1	2.8	−8.1	5 of 46
20	80	8.0	3.6	−8.2	5 of 46
30	70	8.4	4.0	−8.4	5 of 46
40	60	8.7	4.3	−11.3	6 of 46
50	50	9.1	4.7	−14.1	8 of 46
60	40	9.4	5.0	−17.0	11 of 46
70	30	9.7	5.3	−19.8	12 of 46
80	20	10.0	5.5	−22.7	12 of 46
100	0	10.5	6.0	−28.4	12 of 46

Source: The Vanguard Group

balancing act between trying to get the return you want and assuming only the risk you are willing to take. You are aiming for a give and take between two primal emotions: fear and greed.

In the 1950s, Harry Markowitz, the winner of the 1990 Nobel Prize for economics and widely regarded as the founder of modern portfolio theory, began to enlighten investors about the power of asset allocation:

A portfolio of 60 different railway securities would not be as well-diversified as the same size portfolio with some railroad, some public utility, mining, various types of manufacturing, etc. The reason is that it is generally more likely for firms within the same industry to do well or poorly at the same time than [it is] for firms in dissimilar industries.

The importance of the specific industries mentioned more than 50 years ago has of course changed. However, Dr. Markowitz's conclusion that risk averse investors should spread their investments over a variety of asset classes and industries was revolutionary for its time and remains just as relevant today. If your goal is to reduce risk and volatility, broad diversification is extraordinarily important. The relationship between risk and return is the foundation of modern portfolio theory. According to Dr. Markowitz, a trade-off between risk and return exists and investors are well advised to take into account how the performance of one asset class relates to the performance of another asset class when making investment decisions.

Approaches to Asset Allocation

Buy and hold is the most basic approach to asset allocation. As the name suggests, after the initial security purchases are made, you do not make any adjustments. This approach can cause your asset allocation to drift far away from your initial intention. Since there is no rebalancing done, the buy-and-hold approach has no transaction costs after the initial purchases.

In the *insured asset allocation* strategy, you set a floor value whereby if your portfolio drops to that level you become ultraconservative and do not invest anything in equities. You sell stocks as they depreciate, reducing the allocation to them as the portfolio value approaches the floor value. On the other hand, you will buy more stocks if they are appreciating. You become more aggressive as the portfolio rises above the floor value. Insured asset allocation assumes that your risk tolerance changes with your level of wealth. You have no tolerance for risk below the floor value and an increasing risk appetite above the floor value.

The two other main approaches are strategic allocation and tactical allocation. In *strategic asset allocation,* you figure out the percentages of the asset classes you want in your portfolio based on the expected rates of return for those asset classes. If stocks have historically returned 8% annually and bonds have historically returned 4%, a portfolio with a 50% stock and 50% bond allocation would be expected to return 6%, namely, the average of 8% and 4%.

The strategic method of asset allocation is geared toward long-term investors. Here, the mix of assets remains relatively fixed unless your individual circumstances change or there is a shift in your view about the long term behavior of asset classes. A problem with this strategy is that past returns do not necessarily translate into future returns. No one can determine the actual future rates of return of an asset class such as equities on a regular basis. Also brokerage commissions and fees will be triggered when rebalancing occurs. When you move 5% of your assets from bonds into stocks there can be significant transaction costs.

Tactical asset allocation is a more active approach and has a shorter-term focus than strategic asset allocation. You adjust your allocation by examining current market conditions. With this approach, you can engage in deviations from the mix in order to capitalize on perceived investment opportunities. For example, if you feel equities are extremely undervalued because they are trading at a historically low price to earnings ratio, you would raise your stake in stocks relative to bonds and cash. The flexibility of the approach allows you to participate in economic conditions that are more favorable for one asset class than for others. Its goal is to take advantage of perceived inefficiencies in the relative prices of securities in different asset classes. For example, if a Treasury bond is yielding less than a 3-month certificate of deposit (CD), you should adjust your portfolio to have more cash instruments.

Tactical asset allocation requires you to keep an active eye on the markets in search for undervalued and overvalued assets classes. A major weakness of this strategy is that it can trigger a lot of transaction costs and is frowned on by some as a market-timing strategy. Consistently knowing the perfect time to increase or decrease the stake in an asset class is virtually impossible. The advantages and disadvantages of the four asset allocation strategies are summarized in Figure 1.2.

You will probably use both strategic and tactical approaches to asset allocation. Most people use strategic asset allocation to set up their long term goals and then make some tactical changes within that long term framework.

You should not be intimidated by asset allocation. Without realizing it, you already have some experience with asset allocation since you intuitively use these skills to handle your daily finances. For example, shifting money from a savings account into cash before making an outlay for a major purchase is an asset allocation decision. Another example would be a decision to put money into a 3-year CD instead of into a savings account. The difference between the interest rates offered by these products can be a few percentage points. Shopping for the best interest rate on competing financial products is an asset allocation decision that we all make.

When you sit down to allocate your assets, you should follow a set procedure. It is important that you use a logical process and not just make decisions in a random manner. Here are the five steps in allocating your assets:

Step 1: Identify Your Goals and Objectives
Step 2: Choose the Specific Asset Classes in Which to Invest
Step 3: Determine What Percentage of Your Total Assets Belongs in Each Asset Class
Step 4: Decide Which Investment Products to Use
Step 5: Monitor the Performance of Your Portfolio and Adjust Your Asset Mix If Warranted

Figure 1.2 Asset Allocation Strategies: Advantages and Disadvantages

	Buy and Hold	Insured	Strategic	Tactical
Main Advantage	Low transaction costs	Provides downside protection for your portfolio	Disciplined approach to managing your assets	Allows you to take advantage of short term market opportunities
Main Disadvantage	Easy for asset class to become overweighted or underweighted from initial intention	Provides no upside potential once floor is hit	Too much emphasis on past performance of asset classes	High turnover leads to high transaction costs

Step 1: Identify Your Goals and Objectives

You will eventually apply basic financial principles, such as the time value of money, compounding, diversification, economic cycles, and risk versus reward in the process of asset allocation. But the initial step in the process is determining your financial goal. To help guide you during the investment process, you should develop an investment policy statement. You need to write down your investment policy statement; this statement should specifically describe your goals and objectives and how you plan on achieving them. By formally writing down your plan, you're guaranteeing that you'll actually think through what you're going to do. Also, by committing your plan to paper, you have something you can follow in the future and can use as a benchmark when evaluating your progress.

Be realistic. Figure out both the rate of return you hope to earn on your assets and the dollar amount this return will generate. Spell out the risks you are willing to take to get there. There is often a disconnect between what people think they need to achieve to reach a goal and the dollars that are actually required to get there. The investment policy statement should include constraints that are relevant to you, such as your income level, liquidity needs, and your tax situation. You should review your investment policy statement every so often to see if you are on track with your investments. The statement should be modified as circumstances warrant.

The timing of your goals can have a big influence on how your portfolio is structured. If you need money to satisfy important short-term goals that are coming up in the next 5 years, you should be invested conservatively. You should emphasize capital preservation. You want to be sure that you will have the amount of money you need when the time comes in the near future. If you need funds in the long term, 10 or more years from now, you can invest more aggressively. Coming up with a down payment on a house in a year from now would be an example of a short term goal. Having the funds to pay your newborn's entire college tuition is an example of a long term goal. You may have other important goals, such as achieving a reasonable growth of capital and outpacing inflation. If you do not need your money right away, you may be able to take some chances.

It is helpful to segregate investment accounts. For example, having a separate account for retirement savings and another one for a discretionary goal such as a 2-week European vacation is a wise move. Commingling all your assets into one account makes financial planning much more difficult. It will almost automatically cause you not to get all the tax benefits you are entitled to and will not allow you to get the most return for the risk you are willing to take. For example, if the money that you are saving for your retirement is in a regular checking account you would not be receiving the capital appreciation potential and tax benefits offered by an IRA.

While I advise you to open separate accounts for your different objectives, I do not recommend that you wait until the objective pops into your mind to open these accounts. It is dangerous to think like this: first I will save for a house, then for my children's education, and then I will start investing for my retirement. The result of this short term, reactive behavior is that you will not have a penny saved for retirement until you are in your fifties.

The sooner you start saving and investing, the better. You should divide your investment dollars among investment accounts with various goals. At different times, certain accounts will get higher percentages. Only when the goal is accomplished, for example, when the kids finish college and their college tuitions are all paid off, should you stop contributing for that purpose. To accomplish your long-term goals, it is especially important to have investment dollars working that have a chance to compound over the years.

Step 2: Choose the Specific Asset Classes in Which to Invest

The second stage in the asset allocation process is to subdivide the investment universe into specific asset classes, each of which has its own particular risks. It is essential to know what ingredients you have to work with. Different types of investments have different risk and return characteristics. They also react differently to changes in the economic environment, such as inflation and interest rate spikes. Unfortunately, there is no such thing as a risk-free investment that offers tremendous return potential. Smart asset allocation gives you the chance to establish an efficient portfolio. This is one that has the smallest attainable portfolio risk for a given level of expected return or, put another way, the largest expected return for a given level of risk. Your goal as an investor should be to have an efficient portfolio.

Stocks, bonds, and cash are the major asset classes. Real estate and commodities, both in their physical form and as securities, are starting to be included as separate asset classes. Some are even arguing that hedge funds should be considered a separate asset class.

Within all these asset classes, there is a wide gamut of products. It is wise to start with simple products, moving to more complex ones as your knowledge expands and comfort level increases. Understand what you are invested in. In almost all cases, you should have some level of exposure to equities, fixed income, and cash equivalents. Cash equivalents consist of money market funds, certificates of deposit, Treasury bills, cash in currency form, and other short term instruments. You can also make a strong argument that you should have some exposure to real estate, commodities, and international securities in your portfolio.

Do not get boxed into thinking that investments consist of stocks and bonds only. Yes, stocks and bonds should be in pretty much everyone's portfolio, but stocks and bonds do not have to constitute your entire portfolio. By expanding your horizons, you may discover nontraditional investments that provide tremendous return and diversification potential. Following the crowd in your investment decisions is a recipe for mediocre results.

Step 3: Determine What Percentage of Your Total Assets Belongs in Each Asset Class

This step is the most difficult in the process. In deciding how much of your portfolio should be allocated to each asset class, subjectivity comes into play. This decision is more art than science. I say this because if you ask financial professionals how to divide your assets between different asset classes, you will be surprised at how many different answers you get.

I advise you to consider many factors including, but certainly not limited to, age, income, risk tolerance, tax situation, when the money will be needed, and return expectations. The final allocation should have some modicum of diversification so that losses in one asset class can be offset by positive returns in another asset class. You should be able to justify any particular investment you make in a couple of sentences.

For example, a justification for including real estate investment trusts (REITs) in a portfolio is that they provide income and exposure to real estate in a liquid asset.

You should be very mindful about your tolerance for risk. If you are going to be constantly worried about holding a speculative security, it is not wise to own it no matter what the return possibilities. No investment should keep you up at night worrying and possibly causing your health to suffer.

Below are some universal rules that can be applied to your portfolio and serve as a framework for your asset allocation. Your personal circumstance should determine how you incorporate these rules. There is a great deal of wiggle room within these generic rules. For example, a portfolio with 25% in equity and a portfolio with 75% in equity fall within the parameters. The universal rules are:

- You should not have more than 75% in any asset class.
- You should have at least 5% in short term cash instruments.
- You should allocate at least 5% to international securities.
- You should have exposure to at least three asset classes.
- You should hold no more than 10% in an individual stock.
- You should have at least 25% in stocks.
- You should have at least 10% in bonds.
- You should consider rebalancing if an asset class moves at least 5% from its initial weighting.

Once you have decided what percentage of each asset class you want to own, stick with it unless you have sound reasons to change. Be patient. Turn a deaf ear to any investment pundits who claim to know with certainty what the future will bring for the financial markets. Do not be enticed into action by short term market swings. The key question to ask about your allocation is this: will I be able to stick to my investment plan through the market ups and downs that I will inevitably face? You should think about your past reactions to wide market swings.

I remember watching an interview with Mike Tyson when he was in the prime of his boxing career. A sportscaster asked him what strategy should an opponent have who steps into the ring to fight him? Tyson bluntly replied, "Everyone has a plan against me, until they get hit in the face." This boxing analogy can be applied to portfolio management. You should give serious thought *before you invest* to how you will react to a very sharp decline in your assets. Unfortunately, many investors say they have a high tolerance for financial risk until big losses actually happen in their portfolio. That's when they panic and have no plan of action.

One technique that will help you make these all-important allocation decisions is to convert the *absolute dollar value* of your stocks, bonds, and money market funds into percentage terms when determining what asset allocation is right for you. Add up the different asset classes in your portfolio and convert them into percentages. Using percentages makes implementing allocation changes much simpler. It makes it easier to compare your portfolio from one period to another. Whereas 100% is the largest percentage you can have, in dollar terms there is no limit to the amount you can have. The overall pie cannot grow or shrink in percentage terms, while it can in dollar terms from contributions and withdrawals. Instead of trying to decide how much money to place into a given investment, focus instead on the percentage you want there. For example, a target of having 60% in stocks, 30% in bonds, and 10% in cash equivalents is preferable to having a target of $300,000 in stocks, $150,000 in bonds, and $50,000 in cash equivalents.

The Benefits of Diversification

You should never put all your eggs in one basket. The reason is that *diversifying*, or distributing your risk among different baskets, is an easy way to reduce your exposure to risk. Diversification works because different asset classes do not move in perfect tandem with each other. When stocks decline in value, bonds may be rising. When real estate is dropping in value, gold may be hitting record highs. Jim Cramer, the host of *Mad Money* on CNBC, says "diversification is the only free lunch in investing."

Many times certain asset classes react differently to changes in economic conditions. For example, rising interest rates are favorable to cash equivalents while they are generally detrimental to fixed-income securities. Look at the current economic climate in terms of such factors as growth in gross domestic product, where we are in the business cycle, what are the levels of interest rates and inflation, and what is the unemployment rate. This knowledge may influence how you manage your portfolio.

Diversification is not a panacea. It does not guarantee a positive total return over a particular time period. If the majority of asset classes have declining returns, your assets will probably decline in value. You should also be aware that correlations between asset classes change over time. They do not remain static. For example, just because utility stocks have moved in the same direction as Treasury bonds in the past does not mean they will in the future. Figure 1.3 shows the 5-year correlation of different asset classes with large cap domestic stocks. This figure demonstrates how drastically the correlations changed between February 2000 and February 2006.

Diversifying between the major asset classes is not enough. You need to diversify within the asset classes themselves to reduce what is known as *single security risk*, or the risk that your investment will fluctuate widely in value with the price of one holding. In other words, all of the assets you allocate to equities should not be in one stock. Certain stocks and bonds are highly correlated with other stocks and bonds. Others in the same asset class can have very low correlations or possibly a negative correlation. For example, energy and airline stocks many times move in opposite directions. On the fixed income side, Treasury and high yield bonds generally have different return patterns over time.

You can diversify your equity positions in four ways:

1. Buying stocks of different size companies as measured by their market capitalizations: namely, large cap, mid cap, and small cap stocks
2. Buying different styles, such as growth or value stocks
3. Buying in different sectors, such as health care and technology
4. Buying companies domiciled in different countries

Figure 1.3 Correlations of Asset Classes with Large Cap Domestic Stocks in February 2000 and February 2006

Asset Classes	February 28, 2000	February 28, 2006
T-bills	34%	−58%
Long term treasuries	37%	−54%
Commodities	−14%	33%
Small cap stocks	62%	94%
Hedge funds	35%	96%
Non-U.S. stocks	32%	96%

Source: Merrill Lynch

For those who do not want to buy individual stocks, it is easy to get a portfolio spread out over several types of equities by purchasing an equity mutual fund or exchange-traded fund. The number of fund choices has mushroomed over the past decade.

Bond investors can also diversify their portfolios by purchasing bond mutual funds or ETFs instead of individual bonds. Wealthy investors can buy various individual Treasury, corporate, and municipal bonds to diversity their exposure. Bondholders can use techniques such as laddering and weighted maturity/sector strategies that systematically build and maintain a diversified fixed income component to a portfolio.

You also have a number of choices when it comes to cash equivalents. You can choose from various instruments depending on how quickly you need to turn those cash equivalents into cash. A combination of cash, CDs, U.S. Treasury bills, and money market funds constitutes a well-rounded cash position. Cash in currency form is the most liquid while a long term (5-year) CD is the least liquid cash instrument.

You should try to avoid overdiversifying your portfolio and market timing your purchases and sales. They increase your costs and most likely will not add anything to performance. You should try to minimize overlap in your investment holdings. A portfolio with a large percentage of total assets in an S&P 1500 index fund plus a large percentage in an S&P 500 index fund would be an example of a portfolio that has overlap because a large chunk of the S&P 1500 is already composed of S&P 500 stocks.

To have strong performance relative to a benchmark, you need to have some bets in your portfolio. You also have to avoid overdiversification, which will usually result in index-like returns with higher expenses. Free tools available on the Web, such as Morningstar's Portfolio X-Ray can help determine if your portfolio is overdiversified. Morningstar's product examines the holdings of your mutual funds to see if there is a lot of repetition. Portfolio X-RAY not only gives your portfolio's breakdown among stocks, bonds, and cash, but you'll also see what Morningstar investment style box your portfolio belongs in, and how your sector weightings compare with those of the S&P 500. Mutual funds, especially ones with similar objectives, often have many of the same holdings. Be aware that mutual funds are not static; it is possible that they have some different securities from day to day.

Market timing, or knowing when the absolute perfect time to invest in or sell an asset, is impossible. No one knows for sure what the market will bring tomorrow. An investment strategy solely focused on timing the market is an exercise in guessing. However, you can reduce your risk with a technique called *dollar cost averaging*, which entails making automatic contributions to an investment. This places your money in assets in regular amounts and at regular time intervals. You buy fewer shares when prices are high, and you buy a lot when prices are low. Dollar cost averaging helps you avoid the two worst outcomes—buying a lot when the market is at its zenith and selling out of the market when it is at its low point.

Step 4: Decide Which Investment Products to Use

You will need to do some work to choose the specific securities to invest in. You should do some of your own research, no matter what security you choose. Also find out what other brokerage and independent research firms are saying about the security. Never buy a security blindly.

In most of the asset classes, you need to decide whether to invest in individual securities or pools of securities such as mutual funds or some kind of combination of the two. You also need to decide whether to invest in taxable or tax-exempt securities and domestic or international securities. With commodities and real estate, you have the added choice of deciding whether you want to own the actual physical asset: namely, gold ingots or condos in Florida.

Investment consultants and financial planners can help, if you do not feel comfortable allocating your own assets and picking securities yourself. Either way, you should always be extremely cost conscious. High fees and commissions can eat away at your capital and returns.

Financial planning software and questionnaires designed by financial advisors and brokerage firms can be beneficial, but you should never rely solely on a piece of software or a piece of paper with preconceived notions. Remember, many financial institutions like to put their clients into a standardized plan because it's easier for the bank or the brokerage firm, but not necessarily because it's best for their clients. Customization always requires more time and work than mass production. Rules of thumb and questionnaires can give you rough guidelines on how to manage your assets, but do not get cornered into what they tell you. Remember, you are unique and have specific expectations and concerns. Your allocation should not be solely determined by being pigeonholed into a category such as "conservative retiree."

Step 5: Monitor the Performance of Your Portfolio and Adjust Your Asset Mix If Warranted

After you choose your securities, your job is not done. You should periodically monitor how your portfolio is performing. A review should be done at least once during the year, preferably quarterly. An appropriate benchmark should be chosen (for example, the S&P 500 for a large cap stock portfolio) to measure how the portfolio is doing. You also must reassess your allocation when circumstances change in your life: for example, if you get a divorce or if a spouse dies. Buy and hold can be an effective investment strategy; buy and ignore is a recipe for disaster.

When you are evaluating the performance of your assets, you should not just look and see if they are up or down from their initial purchase price. A better approach to judging how your investments have fared is to compare them to relevant benchmarks. There are broad and very narrow benchmarks for each of the major asset classes. The S&P 500, the Lehman Aggregate, and the Citigroup 3-Month T-Bill Index are examples of broad benchmarks that are used to gauge how the overall equity, fixed income, and money market universes are performing. In some cases you may want to dig a little deeper for more relevant comparisons. For example, if you own a small cap mutual fund, the S&P 600 Small Cap Index is a better comparison than the S&P 500. For any benchmark you use make sure that it is measurable, has at least 10 years' worth of history, and is easy to track. Ultimately, if an investment is not performing up to par you want to be able to answer why. Is it a security specific issue or are all similar securities performing the same way?

Major life-changing events such as marriage, having children, and retirement usually require that you shift your mix of assets. You also may have to rebalance your portfolio based on how certain asset classes perform. If an asset greatly outperforms the other assets, it may become overweighted in the portfolio and exceed your initial intention. If an asset class shifts to a 5% higher weighting than you targeted, it is advisable to consider rebalancing.

A major life event or being overweighted in one asset class is a good reason to rebalance your portfolio. You shouldn't rebalance just to rebalance or because you do it every year at the same time. Rebalancing is not free; there are commissions and fees, plus taxes that may be incurred. You should be able to explain why you are rebalancing your portfolio in a few simple sentences. There should be some logic to the action.

Rebalancing is simply the process of realigning the weightings of the asset classes of a portfolio. By rebalancing, you will usually be selling investments that appreciated substantially and buying investments that have underperformed. Although you know that buying low and selling high is a great investment strategy, you will find that it is also one of the hardest to implement. It requires the psychological discipline not to chase your best investments. Just think about it. When you look at your quarterly investment statements and you see the investments that are doing poorly versus the ones that are doing well, what is your first inclination? Is it to get rid of your losers and buy more of your winners? Success in asset allocation may call for doing the opposite and that takes discipline.

When rebalancing your taxable accounts, it is better to use new cash in the implementation instead of selling assets. Contributing new cash to underweighted assets will not incur any tax liabilities. Otherwise, when you rebalance you will be forced to sell some assets causing a taxable event.

For tax-deferred accounts, you can just shift assets around to restore the target allocation since no tax applies. In your 401(k) plan, if you shift 10% of your equity holdings into fixed income, no taxes are incurred. However, there may be some transaction fees that apply if you do this excessively within a calendar year.

You cannot do a good job allocating your assets unless your record keeping is organized. You must have a clear idea of exactly where your money is invested and how much is in each of your accounts. You should also keep duplicate copies of important financial records in a safe location outside of your home, as natural disasters like Hurricane Katrina have demonstrated.

Your investment policy statement should clearly state your asset allocation goal. It is impossible to effectively allocate your assets without knowing exactly what your assets are. There used to be a television ad that asked: "It is 10:00 p.m. Do you know where your children are?"

Anyone who has money invested should have a similar mantra: It is 10:00 p.m. Do you know where your money is?

Dividing Your Assets

How do most people divide up their assets? An example of a generic allocation is displayed in Figure 1.4. This is a common way many people split up their assets. In this pie chart, 60% of the portfolio is placed in equities, 30% is invested in fixed income, and the remaining 10% is invested in cash or cash equivalents. This allocation is a common starting point and is often used as a benchmark to determine how well a balanced portfolio is performing. The benchmark usually has the S&P 500 representing the equity portion, the Lehman Aggregate representing the entire fixed income universe, and the Citigroup 6-Month T-bill representing the cash portion. If you keep this 60–30–10 split, you will have to rebalance your portfolio often. This can result in significant transaction costs.

Once you have established the percentages to put in each of the major asset classes, you need to decide the form in which you will hold

Figure 1.4 Generic Asset Allocation

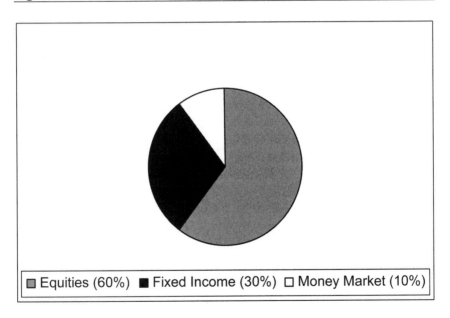

■ Equities (60%) ■ Fixed Income (30%) □ Money Market (10%)

Figure 1.5 Sample Asset Allocation Using Mutual Funds

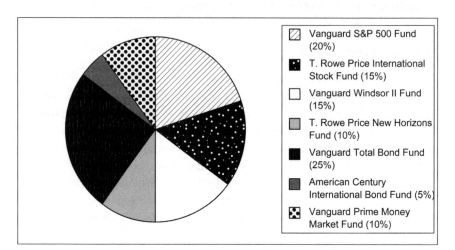

▨	Vanguard S&P 500 Fund (20%)
▪	T. Rowe Price International Stock Fund (15%)
☐	Vanguard Windsor II Fund (15%)
▨	T. Rowe Price New Horizons Fund (10%)
■	Vanguard Total Bond Fund (25%)
▨	American Century International Bond Fund (5%)
▨	Vanguard Prime Money Market Fund (10%)

the assets—mutual funds, ETFs, or individual securities. You will also have to decide whether to use a broker or invest solo. Figure 1.5 shows how the generic asset allocation from Figure 1.4 can be divided. The example uses a combination of active and passive mutual funds offered by large money management firms.

I highly recommend that you do some screening and independent research on specific investments. Do some comparison shopping for yourself. You wouldn't purchase a new car without looking at a few different models, and you should not just blindly buy any financial product. You should do your homework on any potential investment candidate. Understand the return potential and the risk of the security. You should be able to easily explain why you are buying or selling a security. In later chapters, I discuss in much more detail the steps in the asset allocation process that I have outlined in this chapter.

Points to Remember

- Asset allocation is the process of determining the optimal way to divide the broad category of assets in a way that suits your risk and return requirements.

- How you split up your assets between stocks, bonds, and other assets is the most important factor in determining your investment performance.
- Strategic asset allocation has a long term focus and requires you to decide what percentages to put in different asset classes based on their expected returns.
- Tactical asset allocation is more short term focused in that it tries to take advantage of temporary inefficiencies in the relative price of securities.
- You should make sure that your financial house is in order before putting money in the financial markets.
- In your allocation process, you should follow these steps: identify your goals and objectives, choose the asset classes to invest in, determine the percentages within the asset classes for your portfolio, decide on the investment products to utilize, and monitor the portfolio and make adjustments as you see necessary.
- Diversify the asset classes you invest in, as well as within the asset class itself.
- It is key that you ask yourself whether you will be able to stick to your investment plan through the market ups and downs that you will inevitably face.
- Never invest in anything that you do not understand.

CHAPTER 2

ASSET ALLOCATION INGREDIENTS

CHOOSING BETWEEN THE ASSET CLASSES

Don't try to buy at the bottom and sell at the top. It can't be done except by liars.

BERNARD BARUCH

To effectively allocate your assets, you need to know what investment products are best to use. The three main asset classes are stocks, bonds, and cash. Buying stocks for growth and bonds for income and keeping cash or money market funds for safety is too simplistic. A wide array of securities offering different return and risk profiles are available within these asset classes. There is a big difference between the performance you can expect from a U.S. Treasury bond and a high-yield bond issued by a telecom company and between preferred stock offered by General Electric and a micro-cap biotech common stock. In this chapter we look at these asset classes in broad terms and examine their specific segments. History shows that these broad asset classes do not move in tandem. Figure 2.1 shows the performance of stocks, bonds, and cash over the past 10 years.

Equities

In the majority of investment portfolios, equities have the highest weightings of any of the asset classes. They are the sexiest asset class.

Figure 2.1 Yearly Performance History of Stocks, Bonds, and Cash from 12/31/1996 to 12/31/2006

Time Period	Stocks S&P 500 Index, Percent Return	Bonds Lehman U.S. Aggregate Index, Percent Return	Cash Lehman T-Bill Index, Percent Return
12/31/1996			
12/31/1996 to 12/31/1997	31.01	9.65	5.33
12/31/1997 to 12/31/1998	26.67	8.69	5.13
12/31/1998 to 12/31/1999	19.53	−0.82	4.80
12/31/1999 to 12/31/2000	−10.14	11.63	6.08
12/31/2000 to 12/31/2001	−13.04	8.44	4.07
12/31/2001 to 12/31/2002	−23.37	10.26	1.70
12/31/2002 to 12/31/2003	26.38	4.10	1.03
12/31/2003 to 12/31/2004	8.99	4.34	1.23
12/31/2004 to 12/31/2005	3.00	5.26	3.00
12/31/2005 to 12/31/2006	13.62	4.34	4.80
Total returns from 12/31/1996 to 12/31/2006	91.47	88.20	43.84
Annualized returns	6.71	6.53	3.70

Business shows on television often feature talking heads giving their stock picks for the coming months. Stocks come with the lore of high return potential, but they come with high risk and volatility as well. Large company stocks as a group have lost money on average in about 1 out of every 3 years. Between 1926 and 2006, investors have received a premium of about 6.8% to assume the higher risk of stock market investing over the 3-month U.S. Treasury Bill.

Although historically stocks have been a standout performer among different asset choices, there have been pockets of time where their performance was terrible. It took two decades after the 1929 crash for the Dow Jones Industrial Average to go higher than it was before the crash. The period 1970–1982 was characterized by a down market and rabid inflation with the worst year being 1974 when the market was down 30%. Recently, the first few years of the new century had double-digit percentage declines with the biggest pain going to the tech and Internet stocks that were the high flyers of the late 1990s.

Of the major asset classes, equities have provided investors the best inflation protection. Stocks have outpaced inflation—the rising prices of goods and services—over time. Stocks, as represented by the S&P 500, have averaged an annual return of 10.5% over the 80 years ended in 2005. In recent years, small cap stocks have outperformed large caps. For each of the past 7 years, the S&P Small Cap 600 has outperformed the large cap dominated S&P 500. See Figure 2.2.

Companies sell shares of stock to raise money for their operations. When you purchase a stock, you become a part owner of the underlying company. Common shareholders bear the main burden of the risks in a business and also receive the lion's share of the spoils. They have a claim to the earnings and dividends paid out by the corporation. Shareholders generally have voting power, which gives them some say in the way the company is run. Their voting power is in proportion to the number of shares they own. Shareholders usually decide on issues such as who are on the company's board of directors, whether the corporation should accept a takeover bid, and who audits the company's books. Most companies issue common stock, which carries the right to vote; a

Figure 2.2 Yearly Performance History of S&P Indexes from 12/31/1996 to 12/31/2006

Time Period	Percent Return per Period			Cumulative TWR (Basis = 100)		
	S&P 500 Index	Mid Cap 400	S&P Small Cap 600	S&P 500 Index	Mid Cap 400	S&P Small Cap 600
12/31/1996				100	100	100
12/31/1996 to 12/31/1997	31.01	30.44	24.53	131.01	130.44	124.53
12/31/1997 to 12/31/1998	26.67	17.68	−2.09	165.95	153.50	121.92
12/31/1998 to 12/31/1999	19.53	13.35	11.51	198.35	173.98	135.96
12/31/1999 to 12/31/2000	−10.14	16.21	11.02	178.24	202.19	150.94
12/31/2000 to 12/31/2001	−13.04	−1.64	5.73	154.99	198.88	159.60
12/31/2001 to 12/31/2002	−23.37	−15.45	−15.32	118.78	168.16	135.15
12/31/2002 to 12/31/2003	26.38	34.02	37.53	150.11	225.37	185.88
12/31/2003 to 12/31/2004	8.99	15.16	21.59	163.61	259.53	226.01
12/31/2004 to 12/31/2005	3.00	11.27	6.65	168.52	288.77	241.04
12/31/2005 to 12/31/2006	13.62	8.99	14.07	191.47	314.72	274.97
Total returns from 12/31/1996 to 12/31/2006	91.47	214.72	174.97			
Annualized returns	6.71	12.15	10.64			

few companies issue only nonvoting stock; and others may issue several different kinds of stock, a class A and a class B, for example, only one of which carries the right to vote.

Common stocks can be segregated in many different ways. The size of the company and its country of origin are popular ways to divide individual equities. Stocks whose market capitalizations are above 10 billion dollars are considered large cap. Many of these companies are recognizable names such as Microsoft, Coca-Cola, and Boeing. These stocks are considered less risky by some because many have a long history of sales and earnings. They often provide diversity in their product line and solid financials to withstand a downturn in the economy.

Mid and small cap stocks have market capitalizations between $500 million and $10 billion. These companies generally offer higher growth potential along with higher risk than large cap stocks. Since they are starting with a lower base, it is easier for small companies to grow their businesses faster. They often though suffer from being overly reliant on a single product or single customer. In most cases, small cap companies do not have the financial wherewithal that larger companies do. Overall, they have lower credit ratings, less cash, and more debt than large companies.

Foreign stocks have garnered a lot of attention in recent years with their strong performance. Many countries provide greater growth prospects than the United States. Although they have some correlation to the U.S. market, foreign equities do provide diversification benefits. International stocks are generally divided by region and whether they are in established or emerging markets. Examples of regions are Europe, Asia, and Latin America. Economies in countries such as Germany, Japan, and England are considered developed. Many times they list American Depository Receipts of their shares on American exchanges for purchase. These countries have diversified economic bases, established stock exchanges, stable political structures, and an established currency. See Figure 2.3 for a correlation comparsion of various Morgan Stanley Capital International (MSCI) indexes and the S&P 500.

Investing in stocks in emerging markets is more risky than placing money in the United States or Japan. Emerging market economies are less developed, have stock exchanges that sometimes offer questionable liquidity, and often have a great deal of political risk. Countries such

Figure 2.3 Correlation of Various MSCI Indexes with the S&P 500

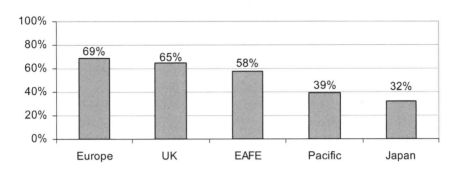

as Russia, China, Brazil, and India would fit the bill as large emerging markets. Thailand, Uruguay, and South Africa are examples of smaller emerging markets. American-style democracies and long histories of free market capitalism are a rarity in the emerging market universe. Corruption and spotty accounting are also commonplace in many emerging markets.

A negative aspect of being an owner of a stock is that in the case of liquidation, common stock shareholders are usually the last in the pecking order of those who receive the proceeds. People who have lent the company money have a higher claim on liquidated assets than owners of the company. In many cases when a company goes bankrupt, the common stockholders end up receiving nothing.

Preferred stock, which not all companies offer, has a higher claim on assets than common shares if a company is liquidated. Preferred stocks usually offer high dividends with small price swings. They have less risk than their common stock brethren and share many characteristics of fixed income securities. Like bonds, many are thinly traded, have wide spreads, and are callable. The capital outlay required to invest in individual preferred shares is lower than with individual bonds and many are taxed at a rate of 15%.

Overall, equities are the most difficult asset class to value. The dividend discount model, relative valuation, and sum-of-parts are a few of the methodologies that analysts use to try to determine the true value of a stock. With the *discount cash flow model* (intrinsic value analysis), estimates of future "free" cash flows are discounted back to current value, incorporating such variables as risk assessment and a company's capital structure. Discounted cash flow models work best with companies that are profitable and tend not to be too cyclical.

Relative valuation assesses a security's value by comparing appropriate financial ratios among its closest peer companies. A problem with this method is that not all industries lend themselves to that kind of comparability. The *sum-of-parts method* tries to determine the "fair value" of a stock by determining private market values for its identifiable, separate units. At their best though, these valuation methods are inexact sciences. Stocks can trade based on rumor and hype and are much more subject to price manipulation than other asset classes. It can take a long time before a stock trades at what its earnings and growth rate suggest. Ultimately, a stock is worth what someone is willing to buy it for at that moment.

From an asset allocation viewpoint, a disadvantage of stocks is that it is virtually impossible to determine what a stock's value will be in the future. Instruments in other asset classes can say with certainty that X number of dollars will give you Y number of dollars in the future. Since stock prices change from second to second you cannot make any kind of guarantee as to what their value will be going forward. Numerous factors can affect what their value will be. The short term risk of equities is much greater than that posed by fixed income and money market instruments.

Brokerage firms and independent research firms such as Standard & Poor's provide *buy*, *sell*, and *hold* recommendations on specific stocks. Analysts from financial firms provide a lot of information and analysis on specific companies and their prospects for the future. An advantage of the recommendations provided by independent research firms is that they have limited conflicts of interest with the specific firms they are covering. Full-service brokerage firms often have investment banking and corporate finance relationships with companies that generate a lot of revenue for their firms. Not surprisingly, the number of "sell" recommendations that brokerage firms give their investment banking clients is miniscule. When making a buy or sell decision try to get at least two opinions from financial firms along with whatever analysis they provide. You should form your own opinion of a stock, but take into consideration what the research community thinks. A well-read and more informed investor is usually a more successful investor.

In my judgment, everyone should have exposure to equities. The growth potential stocks provide should be a component in everyone's overall portfolio. You can choose between a wide variety of stocks. Figure 2.4 shows common ways that stocks are sorted. You can buy equities from small, large, domestic, and foreign companies. You can also base your purchase on different investment styles, such as growth, value, and growth at a reasonable price (GARP), from across all types of industries and businesses. Small companies and foreign companies generally do not offer the liquidity that large blue chip American companies do.

The stock market has become more liquid in recent years for three main reasons: the use of decimals for the pricing of trades on the major stock exchanges, the proliferation of computers and electronic trading, and the increased purchasing of stocks by individuals and institutions. Individuals are beginning to believe that they can get competitive access to equity markets. One result is that a higher percentage of households own stocks in some form than in any other time in history.

The main purpose for holding equities is for growth and capital appreciation. Stocks in industries such as technology and biotech have provided substantial gains to investors over specific time periods. Investors looking for income should not ignore equities either. Stocks in groups such as utilities, real estate investment trusts (REITs), and large money center banks often provide substantial yields. Be aware that equities can have sharp price declines over short periods of time.

A stock's performance is affected by macroeconomic and company-specific factors. The overall economy including interest rate changes, the

Figure 2.4 Types of Equities

Domicile	Size	Style	GICS* Sector
Domestic	Small cap	Growth	Consumer discretionary
Foreign	Mid cap	Value	Consumer staples
	Large cap	GARP	Energy
			Financials
			Health care
			Industrials
			Information technology
			Materials
			Telecom services
			Utilities

*GICS = Global Investment Classification System

inflation rate, employment levels, and gross domestic product growth will affect all stocks. Factors such as recent earnings releases, sales levels, profit margins, and competition are company-specific factors that influence a particular company's stock price. To have good long-term returns, a stock needs both a positive economic environment backdrop for its business and strong company-specific bottom line results.

Bonds

While usually not the subject of much conversation at cocktail parties, bonds are an asset class that should also be in every portfolio. They provide diversification benefits, an income component, as well as a small amount of capital appreciation potential. The name *fixed income security* comes from the fact that most bonds pay a fixed coupon. Bondholders are higher up on the totem pole than stockholders in terms of getting liquidated assets in the case of a bankruptcy of a corporation. As people get older, it is often recommended that they increase the proportion of bonds in their portfolio.

Bonds offer more stability and lower risk than stocks, but have historically had lower total returns and have more inflation risk. Although the long term returns for bonds have been lower than stocks, they should not be dismissed. In many time periods of less than 5 years, bonds have outperformed stocks. Intermediate term government bonds have averaged an annual rate of return of 5.3% over the 80-year period ended in 2006. Especially in declining interest rate environments, bonds perform well.

Bonds are essentially IOUs issued by corporations and governments. The bond issuers promise to pay back the money loaned to them. The enticement to be a lender is that the money loaned is paid back plus interest, usually in the form of coupons. Bonds generally make their cash distributions twice each year.

The standard face value for most bonds is $1,000 or $5,000. Some are issued in larger denominations but few come in smaller ones. They can be purchased though a broker or in the case of Treasuries directly from the government. Prices on more than 20,000 bonds are listed at www.nasdaq.com/trace. After a bond is purchased, it may be traded. The price at which a bond trades may differ from its face value. A bond is said to sell at a premium when the price is above its par (face) value and at a discount when the price falls below it.

Like stocks, the liquidity of the different bond markets has improved over the years and there is a wide assortment of bonds. Bonds can be divided by the type of issuer: usually large companies, state and federal governments, and government agencies. These different entities issue billions of dollars of debt per year.

U.S. Treasury bonds are considered the safest fixed income securities because they are backed by the full faith and credit of the U.S. government. There is little worry that the United States will default on its debt. The U.S. government always has the inflationary option of printing more money. For asset allocation purposes, Treasury bonds provide absolute capital preservation along with a predictable, if modest, rate of return. U.S. Treasury bonds have historically been a safe haven for investors from around the world.

Government agency bonds come with an implied, not absolute, guarantee of paying out their coupon and returning their principal. These bonds are issued by agencies affiliated with the federal government such as the Federal National Mortgage Association (Fannie Mae) and the Student Loan Marketing Association (Sallie Mae). Although the likelihood of default is slightly higher than with Treasury bonds, the chance of these agencies reneging on their obligations is miniscule.

A simple and reasonable way to predict whether a borrower will be able to pay back the principal and interest on its loan is to look at its credit rating. Standard & Poor's and Moody's assign debt ratings to corporate and municipal bonds. Triple A (AAA) is the highest rating assigned by Standard & Poor's to a debt obligation. Figure 2.5 displays Standard & Poor's and Moody's credit rating categories. Credit ratings incorporate such items as debt levels, interest coverage, and cash positions into one specific score. Bonds with higher ratings have a lower chance of defaulting on their debt.

Corporate Bonds

Corporate bonds generally offer higher yields than government bonds because there is more default risk with them. Their ability to pay back their bondholders is determined by the activities and financial status of the issuing corporations. A company can stop paying dividends at any

Figure 2.5 Credit Rating Categories

Investment Grade	S&P's Rating	Moody's Rating
Highest quality	AAA	Aaa
High quality	AA	Aa
Good quality	A	A
Medium quality	BBB	Baa
High-Yield or "Junk" Bonds		
Some speculative elements	BB	Ba
Speculative	B	B
More speculative	CCC	Caa
Highly speculative	CC	Ca
In default	D	—
Not rated	N	N

time, but if it stops paying the interest on its bonds it faces bankruptcy. Individual corporate bonds can be purchased in multiples of $1,000 with a minimum purchase of $5,000. The maturity dates on them can range from 1 year to 40 years.

Companies use the money they collect from these bonds for various business purposes, such as expansion plans and asset purchases. The income of these bonds are fully taxable; they do not have the tax advantages that municipal bonds have. They usually make interest payments twice a year. Corporate bondholders do not have voting rights. They do, however, have priority over preferred and common stockholders in the case of liquidation.

Municipal Bonds

Municipal bonds issued by an entity in your home state are generally free of federal, state, and local taxes. Obviously, such munis should only be held in taxable accounts, and they are best suited to individuals in high tax brackets. If your current federal income tax bracket is 28% or higher, the tax savings on municipal bonds may make them enticing. Many municipal bonds have insurance covering them, decreasing the chance of default. Municipal bond insurance is written by private companies such as Ambac for a fee to issuers hoping to obtain a higher credit rating and to ultimately lower their interest costs.

The two main types of municipal bonds are general obligation and revenue bonds. The main difference between the two is how the revenue to support the bond is generated. General obligation bonds are supported by taxes; revenue bonds are supported by money collected from the use of the project such as highway or bridge tolls.

A caveat of municipal bonds is that some of them could be subject to the alternative minimum tax (AMT), which is entrapping more taxpayers every year. If you are affected by the AMT, the interest from any municipal bond that is for a "private activity" could be taxed even if it is from a public agency. So you need to be wary of bonds that support a hospital, an industrial park, or other projects of that nature. Most bonds specifically state whether they are exempt from the AMT.

Brokers usually require customers to buy individual municipal bonds in at least $5,000 lots. It is unwise to buy them unless you plan to hold them until they mature and the issuer pays back the full face value. If you sell out earlier, you can lose up to 5% of the value of the bond just on the bid/ask spread (the difference between what a broker will sell the bond to you and buy the bond from you).

Maturity of Bonds

Another way bonds can be sorted is by maturity. Short term bonds mature between 1 and 3 years, intermediate term bonds mature between 3 and 10 years, and long term bonds mature after 10 years. Generally, longer term bonds offer higher yields to attract people because they come with more uncertainty risk. This is demonstrated by the yield curve (relationship between the maturity of a bond and the yield of a bond) usually being upward sloping. The investor wants to be compensated for the potentially wider price movements of longer term bonds.

You should be aware that under certain economic conditions the yield curve can be flat (little or no difference between short term and long term securities of the same type) or inverted (short term securities yielding more than long term securities). Flat and inverted yield curves may occur when investors believe that interest rates will fall significantly in the future, causing them to try to lock in the present rates by buying longer term securities.

A factor that can affect the maturity of the bond is if it is callable or noncallable. Some issuers have the option to call (redeem) all their bonds if interest rates drop to a certain level. This would force the bond-holders who were interested in remaining in the bond market to reinvest at lower interest rates. To attract investors, callable bonds need to offer investors higher yields than noncallable bonds.

Zero Coupon Bonds

There are also many types of specialized bonds, including zero coupon bonds, Treasury inflation-protected bonds, convertible bonds, and mortgage bonds. Like their name suggests, zero coupon bonds do not pay a coupon. They sell at a deep discount to their face value and gradually achieve their face value over time. Zero coupon bonds allow you to lock in a relatively assured yield to maturity without having to worry about reinvesting cash interest payments at varying rates in the future. This can be helpful for investors who want to be certain that they have a specific number of dollars in the future for things such as a down payment on a home or a child's tuition.

One catch of zeroes is that income tax is owed on the implicit interest that accrues each year. If you hold these bonds in taxable accounts, you have to pay taxes on money not yet received. These bonds are also the most volatile of any bonds in their respective credit quality and maturity range because they pay no interest to cushion the blow of any change in interest rates.

Treasury Inflation-Protected Securities

Treasury Inflation-Protected Securities (TIPS) protect you against one of the biggest risks in bonds: inflation risk. Since the start of 1960, the Consumer Price Index (CPI) has risen an average of about 4% a year and has been a positive number every year. TIPS pay a coupon and their principal value is adjusted every 6 months to match the Consumer Price Index. In the event that there is deflation, the U.S. Treasury has guaranteed that they will repay at least the face value of the inflation-protected bond.

These securities can be purchased from the U.S. Treasury in January, July, and October. TIPS can be bought through Treasury Direct at www.publicdebt.treas.gov. Also, mutual funds such as the Vanguard Inflation-Protected Securities Fund (VIPSX) provide an inexpensive exposure to TIPS. It's better to hold TIPS in a tax-sheltered account because the annual payments will otherwise be taxed as ordinary income, even though you do not actually receive the inflation-adjusted additions to principal until the bond is redeemed.

Convertible Bonds

Convertible bonds give bondholders exposure to stocks. The bonds carry the option of conversion into equity of the issuing company. When the underlying stock rises, these bonds benefit. Since they have this convertibility feature, they offer a lower interest rate than regular issues of comparable quality and maturity. The average yield on these bonds is about 4%. They have returned an average of 13% over the past 10 years. Convertible bonds provide a way to receive income from sectors of the equity market that normally do not have high dividend yields such as technology stocks.

When a convertible bond is purchased it is given a conversion ratio. This simply states how many shares of stock the bond can turn into $1,000. A conversion ratio of 50:1 means the bond can be converted into 50 shares of stock at a price of $20 each. If the stock never reaches the conversion price the bond cannot be turned into stock. The bond though does continue to produce income.

Mortgage Bonds

A mortgage bond is a bond secured by a mortgage on a property. Such bonds are backed by real estate that can be liquidated. Mortgage bonds have an added risk factor called *prepayment risk* that gives them a higher yield than similarly rated government bonds. Mortgage bonds can be prepaid for voluntary reasons such as the borrower has the money to pay off the loan and involuntary reasons such as bankruptcy and foreclosure. When bonds are prepaid, bondholders who want to get back into the bond market usually have to do so at lower yields.

International Bonds

You can diversify your fixed income holdings by buying some foreign bonds, in the same way that you buy foreign stocks. During periods when the U.S. bond market may be floundering, international bonds can be performing well. The large budget and trade deficits that the United States currently has make foreign debt look like an attractive option. If these twin deficits continue, the dollar will depreciate over the long term, increasing the value of foreign currencies and subsequently their bond prices.

International bonds come with some of the same concerns as foreign stocks: political risk, currency risk, and liquidity issues. Like domestic bonds, they are also highly affected by the interest rate environment in their home country. High and rising interest rates are not good for any bonds no matter where they are located.

You can buy international corporate and/or government bonds. It is recommended that you buy foreign bonds via a mutual fund or ETF. Purchasing a fund will give you some diversification, professional management, and liquidity. Aim to buy a no-load fund with an expense ratio below 1.

Cash Instruments

The safest and most liquid of all the major investing classes is cash and money market instruments. Cash encompasses such assets as currency, checking and savings accounts, Treasury bills, and short term certificate of deposits. Typically, investors rely on these assets to store money they will need for emergencies and short term goals. Cash provides the best short-term capital preservation component of the major asset classes. It can also be used as part of an investment strategy if you expect interest rates to rise and as a parking place for cash while deciding on an investment or other large expenditure.

Cash and money market fund assets carry very little risk but also struggle to outpace inflation over time. According to Ibbotson Associates, cash (as represented by Treasury bills) averaged an annual rate of return of 3.6% over 80 years ended in 2006. For investment purposes, cash generally comes in three forms: money market accounts, money market mutual funds, and certificates of deposits (CDs). You should factor in your time horizon and feelings about the direction of interest rates in deciding which cash instruments to employ.

Money market mutual funds are a type of mutual fund that invests in short term debt instruments, including government paper, commercial paper issued by corporations, and bank certificates of deposit. They were initiated in 1973 when short term interest rates were at record levels. Some of these funds invest exclusively in Treasury securities and others in tax-exempt securities, and they are offered by all the major brokerage houses and mutual fund families. These accounts are mainly used by people with brokerage accounts who sell a stock and then put the proceeds in a money market fund until they decide where to reinvest the cash. Money market funds allow you to write checks and make electronic transfers, but most accounts require you to maintain a minimum dollar amount.

Brokers and mutual fund families commonly offer single-state municipal bond money market funds, which pay income that's tax-free at the state as well as the federal level. Tax-free options are not available with CDs. The expense ratio charged on competing money market mutual funds must be considered because the return provided by these products is limited.

While CDs and money market accounts are covered by the Federal Deposit Insurance Corporation up to $100,000 per deposit per institution, the FDIC or any other government agency does not guarantee money market mutual funds. Money market funds try to preserve the value of their investments at $1.00 per share. Although it is extremely rare, it is possible to lose money by investing in these funds. There has been only one case of a fund actually "breaking the buck" (meaning that its share price dipped below $1), and in that case the fund company made good on any losses to investors.

The value of your principal does not fluctuate with a CD. Also the interest rate will remain the same until the maturity date of the CD. Be aware, owning certificates of deposits can result in a loss to you if they are not held to maturity. If you withdraw money from a CD early, you are penalized and this can result in a negative return for the asset. Money market accounts and money market funds allow you to withdraw your money at any time and often offer lower yields than CDs for that convenience.

The yield on money market funds and accounts will fluctuate depending on the direction of interest rates, while the rate on a CD stays fixed. It logically follows that money market funds and accounts benefit in a rising interest rate environment and CDs have better relative performance in a declining rate environment.

There are several good sources to help you find competitive interest rates on cash instruments. On the Internet, www.bankrate.com and www.iMoney.net.com collect information weekly from financial institutions and create a list of the best rates nationwide or in just one specific state for money market and savings accounts. Another good website is www.money-rates.com, which provides rates for different financial companies plus links to their specific sites. Most local newspapers also provide tables of the interest rates offered by local banks each week. Figure 2.6 shows examples of high-yielding cash instruments on a few different vehicles as of mid 2007. As you can see, many times the best rates are offered by smaller, less well-known financial institutions.

Besides the three major asset classes, you can invest your money in alternative asset classes. Two that have begun to enter many portfolios are real estate and commodities, and I discuss them later in the chapter. In recent years, they gave garnered a lot of attention because of their strong performance. Hedge funds, which have also received a lot of recent attention, should not be considered a separate asset class.

Figure 2.6 Rates for Certificates of Deposits and Money Market Accounts*

Institution	Rate	APY†	Minimum Deposit
1-Month Certificates of Deposit			
Beal Bank Nevada	4.94	5.05	$1,000
Virtual Bank	4.88	5.00	$10,000
Heritage Bank, N.AB	4.74	4.83	$1,000
Lasalle Bank	3.83	3.90	$2,000
1-Year Certificates of Deposit			
Ascentia Bank	5.37	5.50	$500
Pacific Mercantile Bank	5.32	5.46	$10,000
Indymac Bank	5.31	5.45	$1,000
La Jolla Bank	5.27	5.40	$10,000
Money Market Accounts			
Ascentia Bank	5.27	5.40	$100,000
Bank of Wausau	5.23	5.35	$25,000
GMAC Bank	5.16	5.30	$500
Apple Bank	5.14	5.27	$1

*Data from money-rates.com and bankrate.com
†APY = Annual percentage yield

Hedge Funds

Hedge funds are pools of assets that mainly hold stocks, bonds, or derivations of them. Currently, there are about 9,000 hedge funds and the entire industry has about $1.34 trillion under management.

Most hedge funds seek to profit by pursuing leveraging and other speculative investment practices that may increase the risk of investment loss. They are structured as limited liability partnerships that are only open to the relatively wealthy. In most cases, investors must have a net worth of $1 million or higher or an annual income in excess of $200,000 for the past 2 years to be eligible to invest in an individual hedge fund.

Hedge funds have a limited number of shareholders, and regulatory oversight of them is very limited. Currently, hedge funds are not required to register with the SEC. One justification for the lack of regulation is that the people who invest in hedge funds are sophisticated investors who should be able to fend for themselves. It is still worthy to note that more than 50 hedge funds have come under federal scrutiny for bilking investors of more than $1 billion over the past 5 years.

For the most part, hedge funds are aggressive mutual funds with higher fees and less liquidity. They use a large assortment of investment strategies. They employ techniques such as shorting and the buying and selling of options and futures that most portfolios do not use, but this doesn't merit them being a separate asset class.

Hedge funds possess two big problems for use in asset allocation. First, they are not generally in one single asset class, making them difficult to classify. Second, many hedge fund managers refuse to discuss their strategy because they do not want to reveal the market inefficiency that they are trying to exploit. If you do not know with what assets and in which way a portfolio is being managed, how can you feel comfortable employing hedge funds in an asset allocation strategy?

Real Estate

Real estate has created a tremendous amount of wealth and garnered a lot of media attention over the past few years. As the saying goes, "God only created so much land." Historically low mortgage rates, tight supply in many markets, and strong demand have fueled tremendous gains in real estate prices. For most Americans, their home is the biggest single investment they have. A huge plus of physical real estate is that you can receive enjoyment and utility out of it. That cannot be said for a physical share of IBM stock or a U.S. Treasury bond.

A common practice in real estate investing is to purchase a property such as a home or office with the intent of renting it out. By having tenants, investors can benefit from the rental income as well as any capital appreciation to the property. Some inflation protection is provided because rising operating costs can be passed on to the tenants.

Besides owning physical real estate, you can gain exposure to this asset class at a fraction of the cost by purchasing real estate investment trusts. A real estate investment trust (REIT) is a corporation or trust that uses the pooled capital of many investors to purchase and manage income property (equity REIT) and/or mortgage loans (mortgage REITs). REITs as an investment class have been one of the standouts in the equity market over the past few years. The Wilshire Real Estate Securities Index had an annualized return of 28.2% for the past 3 years and has substantially outperformed the S&P 500 since 2000.

REITs are more liquid than actual physical real estate since they are traded on stock exchanges every business day of the year. You don't have to be concerned with real estate brokers, closing costs, and title searches. By owning several properties, often in different regions, a REIT's risk can be spread out geographically. A major layoff in a town where one property is does not mean that another property owned in the REIT that is 150 miles away will be affected.

Unlike corporations, REITs do not have to pay income taxes if they meet certain Internal Revenue Service Code requirements. To receive the benefit, a REIT must distribute at least 90% of its taxable income to its shareholders and receive at least 75% of that income from mortgages, rents, and sales of property. The result is that they tend to have high dividend yields; the average yield of a REIT is currently about 5.5%. This makes them an attractive option for individuals looking for income from their investments.

They also provide a good inflation hedge and low correlations to the other asset classes. According to Standard & Poor's, between 1970 and 2006 the correlation between REITS and large cap stocks, small cap stocks, and long term bonds were all between 0.20 and 0.30 indicating that adding REITs to a portfolio provided significant diversification benefits.

The main risk with Equity REITs is that the markets where the underlying properties are located may turn sour, reducing the demand and ability of renters to make their payments. The main concern for mortgage REITs is that high and climbing interest rates levels would reduce mortgage demand and have an adverse affect on borrowers' ability to pay back loans.

Commodities

Commodities are another alternative asset class that has attracted investors recently with strong performance of some of its components. Gold and oil have recently reached their highest levels in 20 years. Commodities are generic, largely unprocessed goods that can be processed and resold. They are bulk goods such as grains, metals, and foods that are traded on a commodities exchange or on the spot market. Exposure to commodities can be gained through spot or futures markets. *Spot* being the price now; the *futures* simply being the price at an upcoming date.

Real returns over inflation, diversification benefits, and appealing exposure to economic and demographic trends are reasons to consider making room for commodities in your portfolio. Supply is limited in many commodities and demand has been growing steadily with big pushes from emerging economic powerhouses China and India with their billion-plus populations.

Although commodities are a bit more volatile than equities, they offer impressive correlation benefits. They have demonstrated low or even negative correlation with stocks and bonds. Commodities have demonstrated a desirable tendency to appreciate when financial asset prices are falling. One of the main reasons for the lack of correlation is that inflation erodes the value of financial assets even as hard assets appreciate.

To invest in commodities, you do not have to take delivery of pork bellies or gold bullion. You can invest in diversified indexes such as the Standard & Poor's–Goldman Sachs Commodities Index (S&P-GSCI) and the Dow Jones–AIG Commodities Index (DJ-AIGCI). The S&P-GSCI, a broad benchmark for commodity returns based on commodity futures markets, produced a total return of 9.0% annualized for the 15-year period ending in December 2006. If you measure from the end of 1969, which includes the inflationary 1970s, the index has provided an annualized return of 11.9%. The S&P-GSCI is composed of 24 exchange-traded futures contracts: six energy products, five industrial metals, eight agricultural products, three livestock products, and two precious metals. The index focuses on having adequate liquidity and is production weighted, which results in a high exposure to energy. Crude oil comprises close to 36 percent of the index.

The Dow Jones–AIG Commodities Index is an arithmetically calculated price index composed of futures contracts on 20 physical commodities. The trading activity of a particular commodity helps determine its weight in the index. To ensure diversification, no related group of commodities is allowed to constitute more than 33 percent of the index, and no single commodity may constitute less than 2 percent.

These commodity indexes have three sources of return potential: price, roll, and collateral. Price return comes from changes in commodity futures prices. When the spot price rises, so does the future price in general, producing a positive price return. Roll return comes from rolling long futures positions forward through time. In the futures market, when the spot commodity price exceeds the futures price (backwardation), a long position in a future contract will earn a positive roll return because arbitrageurs ensure that the future price will rise to equal the spot price at maturity. Collateral return comes from the interest when 100% of the collateral is invested in Treasury bills.

You can also get commodity exposure by buying stocks of companies that produce or sell commodities such as gold stocks like Newmont Mining (NEM) or a copper stock like Phelps Dodge (PD). You should be aware that owning individual commodity stocks doesn't provide as low a correlation to other asset classes as buying a commodity index. There are also an assortment of mutual funds and exchange-traded funds with commodity themes. Some ETFs such as StreetTracks Gold (GLD), iShares Silver (SLV), and the United States Oil Fund (USO) directly track the prices of specific commodities

You should also be cognizant that there are heavy tax burdens placed on physical investments in bullion and bullion-backed ETFs. Gold investments are considered collectibles by the IRS, and if they are held for more than 1 year they are taxed at the long term capital gains rate of 28%, instead of the usual 15%.

Investors in commodities should only do business with registered firms. Make every effort to avoid scam artists. All legitimate brokerages must be registered with the National Futures Association which has a list of all complaints, sanctions, and arbitrations involving the firm.

Collectibles

Collectibles are a broad asset class encompassing objects such as fine art, coins, and stamps. With the advent of the Internet and auction websites such as eBay, it has become easier to buy and sell collectible items. Anyone with access to an Internet connection is a possible global player in this market. It is recommended that individuals have no more than 5% of their investable assets in collectibles. People who want to have some money in this asset class should choose a collectible in a market they understand and one that they have a passion for.

Storage and preservation of the items is a concern but the major negative with collectibles is their lack of liquidity. It is difficult to quickly get cash for these items. The market for the majority of collectibles is small, with a limited number of buyers and sellers. It is also tough to get an accurate measure of a collectible's value. What a price guide might say an item is worth can sometimes be very different from what you can actually get for it. There are a lot of unscrupulous characters in the collectible universe. You need to try your best to deal with reputable buyers and sellers in this market.

Before putting money in any asset class described in this chapter, you should have a good understanding of its characteristics. You need to know the pluses and minuses of each of them. This knowledge will help you manage your portfolio during the peaks and valleys that are certain to come in the future.

Points to Remember

- The ingredients for managing your money are stocks, bonds, cash instruments, real estate, commodities, and collectibles.
- There are many choices within each of these asset classes.
- Securities within asset classes can be segregated by size, taxability, and country of origin.
- Hedge funds are not a separate asset class.

- Stocks provide growth and income potential with some risk.
- Fixed income securities usually provide more income, lower returns, and less risk than equities.
- Cash instruments provide stability and a small yield.
- Real estate provides income, capital appreciation potential, and diversification benefits.
- Commodities provide capital appreciation potential and some inflation protection.
- Collectibles provide capital appreciation potential but have poor liquidity.

CHAPTER 3

THE PACKAGING OF THE ASSET CLASS

Our favorite holding period is forever.

WARREN BUFFETT

You can buy financial assets in many different forms. For example, you can get exposure to General Electric stock in many ways—you can buy General Electric's common stock, preferred stock, call or put option, or you could buy a mutual fund or ETF that holds it. The wrapping that goes around an investment product can make the difference between whether it is appropriate or inappropriate for you. There is a big difference between the risk and reward potential of a call option on a stock and a diversified mutual fund. You are lucky today to have a variety of ways to buy into the capital markets. Ultimately, choice is good for consumers.

Individual Securities

The instrument that has been around the longest in the stock and bond markets is the individual security. While many people think security refers to stocks, the term *security* refers to both stocks (also called *equities*) and bonds (also called *fixed income securities*). Individual securities are what all financial products are built around. The individual stock or bond offers higher return potential along with higher risk than a pooled assortment of these securities. For example, IBM stock is more volatile than the Fidelity Magellan Fund. By their very nature individual stocks and bonds are subject to single security risk because in isolation they do not take part in the benefits of diversification.

The individual security is subject to the specific risks of its underlying issuer. If a company reports poor earnings numbers or its bond rating is downgraded to junk status, the price of its issued stocks or bonds will certainly be affected.

Holding a single stock rather than a perfectly diversified portfolio increases annual volatility by roughly 30%. To get full diversification by using only individual securities, you would need to purchase at least 25 separate securities. This way of constructing a portfolio would generate a lot of brokerage commissions and be inefficient for someone who does not have a lot of capital. You should target putting in at least $2,500 for each individual stock purchased. Investing less than this amount is not very efficient. Brokerage costs are more expensive percentagewise the lower the dollar amount you invest.

Owning single securities gives you some degree of control. You have the option to take possession of the physical security even though most of us defer the responsibility of custody to our brokerage firm. You also have the right to vote by proxy on some corporate matters. It also allows you to control the entire investment decision. If the stock or bond goes up or down, you can decide whether you want to buy, sell, or hold. With a portfolio of securities such as in a mutual funds or ETF, you cannot control whether a fund manager buys or sells a specific security within the fund. You only have the decision power of whether you want to buy or sell the fund as a whole.

Individual bonds offer the benefit of a set maturity date and coupon rate. Unlike investors in bond mutual funds or ETFs, investors in individual bonds know that on a set date they are going to get their principal. They can also be certain that during interim periods they are going to receive a certain dollar amount in coupons as long as the bond isn't called or doesn't go into default.

Derivatives

A *derivative* is an investment whose value is based on or "derived" from the value of another security. The instrument allows you to leverage your investment ideas by putting a little money down for the chance of receiving substantial gains. With many derivatives, there is the possibility that you lose all the money you put in the investment. In isolation, these are high-risk investments with high return potential. Derivatives, though, used in combination with other securities in a portfolio can reduce risk, better ensure gains, and increase the income generated from an asset.

Options are a common form of derivative security. The market for publicly traded options has exploded. Today, more than a million options contracts change hands on the Chicago Board Options Exchange every day, and that represents less than half of the market. Each options contract usually represents 100 shares of a stock, so the market is even bigger than it seems.

Assets for which there are option contacts include many individual stock issues, U.S. Treasury bonds and notes, various indexes, various Treasury and Eurodollar obligations, and certain stock index futures contracts. Options give you the right but not the obligation to purchase or sell a security at a predetermined price. *Call options* give the buyer the option to buy a security, while *put options* give the option to sell a security. Purchasers of call options hope the underlying security goes up in value, while buyers of put options hope the underling security declines in value.

The three main components of an option are its underlying security, its strike or exercise price, and its time to maturity. The *underling security* is the financial asset which the option is derived from. The *strike price* is the price at which you can purchase the underlying security. Lastly, the *maturity* of the option defines the time period within which you can buy or sell the security at the exercise price. Most options can be exercised up to and including their maturity date (American options). European options give less flexibility to you because they can only be exercised at their maturity date. These names have no relationship to where the options are trading. Both American and European options trade on exchanges and over the counter in the U.S., Europe, and throughout the world. Options are sometimes referred to as *wasting assets*. This reflects the fact that as they near expiration, they lose more and more of their time value.

When the price of the underlying security in a call option goes above the strike price, it is considered *in the money*. The opposite is true for a put option; it is *in the money* when the underlying security goes below the strike price.

Options can be used for various purposes. For investors who think a security is going to shoot up in price in the short term, call options provide a way to make a lot more money than by just purchasing the individual stock. Investors who feel a stock is going to get hammered in the short term can make more money by buying a put option than by shorting the stock. With their leverage, options in isolation are the epitome of a high-return and high-risk investment. The SEC has captured many traders using inside information by their buying and selling of options. Red flags are raised to law enforcement when investors who do not dabble in the stock market very much buy significant amounts of options on a security.

Investors who have bought a stock that has appreciated since purchase can lock in the gain with the use of options. By selling a call option with a strike price between the current price of the stock and the original purchase price plus the option price, an overall gain is assured. Also, by not having to sell the appreciated stock, one avoids capital gains tax.

Options can also be used to generate income. The primary method for doing this is selling call options, which is also referred to as *covered call writing*. Covered call writing involves selling one call option for every 100 shares of stock that is owned. The premium that is received for selling the options provides income and can increase your rate of return.

Another popular derivative product is futures contacts. A *futures contract* is an exchange-traded, standardized agreement providing for the future exchange of a financial asset or commodity at an agreed-upon price on a specified date. A futures contract obligates the seller to sell the underlying financial instrument or commodity and the buyer to purchase it at the predetermined price on the settlement date, unless the contract is sold to another before. Sometimes this may happen if a trader waits to take a profit or cut a loss. This contrasts with option trading, in which the option buyer may choose whether or not to exercise the option by the exercise date. The value of the futures contract will fluctuate as the price of the underlying financial asset or commodity changes. If you choose, the contract can be sold to close out the position.

Mutual Funds

A mutual fund is a type of investment product that gathers assets and invests them in individual stocks, bonds, or money market instruments more efficiently than individuals could. Essentially, the funds pool money and with the proceeds buy a number of securities and then divide them into individual shares. Mutual funds can meet your diverse needs and objectives with a whole host of strategies.

The mutual fund as a vehicle for investment has become extremely popular over the past 20 years. The amount of money invested in mutual funds over the last 75 years is shown in Figure 3.1.

Interestingly, mutual fund assets declined substantially in their early days because of the Great Depression and lack of confidence in the capital markets and have grown exponentially in recent years. Today there are more mutual funds than stocks listed on the New York Stock Exchange.

The majority of mutual funds are *open-end funds*, in which the amount of shares issued can change depending on inflows into the fund. Open-end funds are not traded on an exchange, but are purchased from and redeemed by the mutual fund company itself. The price of the shares fluctuates daily, corresponding with the value of the securities in the portfolio.

Closed-end funds are investments where the amount of shares is fixed. Listed on exchanges, closed-end funds sometimes trade at a discount or premium to the value of the actual holdings in the portfolio. The supply of and demand for the fund helps explain the spread between the price of the fund and its underlying assets.

Benefits of Mutual Funds

A main benefit of mutual funds is that they provide professionally managed diversified portfolios at a reasonable cost. Most investors do not have sufficient capital to properly diversify by purchasing individual

Figure 3.1 Money Invested in Mutual Funds, 1929–2004

Year	Mutual Fund Investments
1929	$3 billion
1940	$450 million
1960	$17 billion
1985	$500 billion
2004	$8 trillion

securities. Mutual funds are required by the SEC to hold more than 20 securities, allowing investors to get some modicum of diversification. The majority of funds hold many securities across many different business lines which spreads the risk around. Funds that invest exclusively in a single sector or a specific country offer less of a diversification benefit. These narrowly focused funds though do provide more diversification than a single individual stock or bond.

Mutual funds can be purchased at a reasonable cost (which will be discussed in more detail in Chapter 5) and offer the benefit of a full-time professional money manager. Most people are busy with their lives and would rather farm out the buying and selling of securities to a professional. Mutual funds are managed by individuals whose sole job is managing money; they look to buy underpriced securities and to sell overpriced ones. Money managers often have extensive work and educational backgrounds and the resources of their firm to help them in getting investment ideas and making portfolio decisions. Providing an incentive for portfolio managers, a big chunk of their compensation is often tied to how their fund performs relative to similarly classified funds.

Convenience is another one of the major benefits of mutual funds. The *net asset value* (NAV), the price of the mutual fund, is calculated once per day at the market close and is published in major newspapers the following day. Most funds can be opened up with less than a $3,000 investment. They can be purchased over the phone, on the Internet, through traditional mail, or in person at a branch office. The funds can be set up so that deposits are automatically deducted from a checking account, wired into the company, or mailed in, usually with prepaid postage. The fund company also handles the book and record keeping of all the transactions of the fund which would be a Herculean task for an individual investor to do. Furthermore, if you have any questions about your fund account, the major money management companies have 1-800 phone numbers where you can talk to a customer service employee. The fund companies have extensive websites on which you will find answers to many investor queries.

Regulation of Mutual Funds

U.S. mutual funds are subject to strict regulation from the Securities and Exchange Commission. The agency makes sure that mutual funds comply with four federal laws: the Securities Act of 1933, the Securities Exchange Act of 1934, the Investment Company Act of 1940, and the Investment Advisers Act.

The Investment Company Act has the most direct influence on a mutual fund's operations. It regulates the structure and operation of mutual funds and requires funds to safeguard their portfolio securities and keep detailed books and records. It also requires all prospective fund investors to receive a prospectus containing full disclosure of the fund's management, holdings, fees and expenses, and performance.

The National Association of Securities Dealers oversees most mutual fund advertisements and marketing material. The Internal Revenue Code sets requirements regarding a fund's diversification and its distribution of earnings. Mutual funds also have directors who are responsible for extensive oversight of the fund's policies and procedures. For most funds, at least 75% of their directors and the chairman of the fund board must be independent of the fund's management.

In recent years, despite all these regulations, some mutual fund companies have not been Boy Scouts. There have been cases where stocks were touted to investors publicly while they were being dumped by the money management firm privately. Unfortunately, engaging in illegal and unethical acts and putting their own interests ahead of their shareholders occurred at more than a few token financial companies. Mutual fund firms such as Putnam, Janus, and Strong had their reputations severely tarnished.

A widespread unethical act that occurred was "market timing," which involves short term in-and-out trading of mutual fund shares. It is designed to exploit the market inefficiency when the NAV of the mutual fund shares set at the market close does not reflect the current market value of the securities held by the fund. This became especially prevalent for international funds whose funds were priced at a time the actual securities were trading ahead of that time. This created an arbitrage opportunity for market timers who were able to obtain a riskless profit when they bought mutual funds at the stale NAV and sold the shares the next day at the funds' true value. Mutual fund companies state in their prospectuses that they discouraged or prohibited this activity, but clearly some allowed it to occur. To dissuade market timers, many money management firms have implemented special redemption fees for mutual shares held less than a certain amount of time, usually 90 days.

An illegal practice under SEC rules that occurred was late trading or "after hours trading." This involves placing orders for mutual fund shares after the 4 p.m. close but still getting that day's closing price, rather than the next day's closing price. Some mutual funds allowed some hedge funds and large clients to engage in this activity. New York Governor Eliot Spitzer likened late trading to "betting on yesterday's horse races." When deciding on putting money with a mutual fund family, stay clear of companies that do not uphold to the highest ethical standards. There are many quality mutual funds you can choose from, so why place your money with a firm that exhibits dubious behavior.

Types of Mutual Funds

There are a wide variety of mutual funds available for purchase. Professionally managed funds run by well-known portfolio managers, as well as ones that are tracked to an index are offered to investors by financial firms. Some funds have as little as $10 million while others have billions of dollars invested in them. Firms such as Morningstar and Standard & Poor's give investment opinions on funds that can help individuals compare similar offerings.

Funds of all the major asset classes can be bought, as well as balanced or hybrid funds that combine more than one asset class in a single portfolio. Funds that shift the allocation of their asset classes as a target date approaches have recently been added to many mutual fund company offerings. Mutual fund companies such as Fidelity, Vanguard, and T. Rowe Price offer such asset allocation funds.

Equity Mutual Funds

For the most part equity funds can be distinguished by their investment style, the sector that predominates, or the country or region where most of the securities are domiciled. Investment style usually breaks down into whether a manager uses a growth, value, or growth at a reasonable price (GARP) style and whether the selections are mainly large, mid, or small cap stocks (see Figure 3.2).

There are many mutual funds that do not neatly fit into a style paradigm. Be aware also that sometimes funds change their style. Moreover, just because the fund's title states that it is the XYZ Large

Figure 3.2 Major Investment Styles

Style	Size of Holdings	Size of Holdings	Size of Holdings
Growth	Small cap	Mid cap	Large cap
GARP	Small cap	Mid cap	Large cap
Value	Small cap	Mid cap	Large cap

Cap Value Fund doesn't necessarily mean that the equities it selects are in fact in that category. For example, more than 100 mutual funds classified as U.S. stock funds now have more than 20% of their portfolios in non-U.S. securities, according to Morningstar. Go through the prospectus and materials distributed by the money management company to see what type of strategy the fund has and verify that they are abiding by it. Know what you are buying.

More appropriately, equity funds are sometimes grouped by their main financial objective. Looking at equity funds based on the funds goal is helpful in setting up a portfolio and doing an asset allocation. Aggressive growth and growth and income are two classifications that are often used. The Mutual Fund Education Alliance classification of equity funds follows. Different classifications of stock mutual funds are listed along with their investor suitability. Examples of some no-load funds in these classifications are also included. The mutual funds listed are just examples; they should not be viewed as investment recommendations. All equity funds will provide the benefit of some diversification and the potential for return enhancement and risk reduction, especially to portfolios that do not have a large exposure to stocks.

There are six types of equity mutual funds, and each type is suitable for a particular kind of investor.

1. **Aggressive Growth Funds:** These funds invest in common stocks with a high potential for rapid growth and capital appreciation. They often invest in small emerging companies and seek to maximize growth of capital. These funds can experience wide swings up or down. Some use borrowing, short-selling, options, and other speculative strategies to leverage their results.
   - **Suitable for:** Investors who can assume the risk of potential loss in value of their investment in the hope of achieving large gains. They are not suitable for conservative investors

who must preserve their principal or who must maximize current income.

- **Examples:** T. Rowe Price New Horizons Fund, Vanguard Explorer Fund, Fidelity Aggressive Growth Fund

2. **Growth Funds:** These funds invest in stocks for their growth potential rather than their dividend potential. They mainly invest in well-established companies that have good long term records. Growth funds provide low current income, but the investor's principal is more stable than it would be in an aggressive growth fund.

  - **Suitable for:** Growth-oriented investors willing to take risk, but not as much as in aggressive growth funds. They are not for investors seeking to maximize current income.
  - **Examples:** Vanguard U.S. Growth Fund, T. Rowe Price Blue Chip Growth Fund, Fidelity Blue Chip Growth Fund

3. **Growth and Income Funds:** These funds seek long term growth of funds as well as current income. The investment strategy for reaching these goals varies. Some funds invest in a combination of securities, dividing them between those with high dividends and those with high yields. Other funds look for individual stocks that combine both growth and income characteristics. Others may invest in growth stocks and earn current income by selling covered call options on their portfolio of stocks.

  - **Suitable for:** Investors who can assume some risk to achieve growth of capital but who also want to maintain a moderate level of current income.
  - **Examples:** TIAA CREF Growth & Income Fund, Fidelity Growth & Income Fund, T. Rowe Price Growth & Income Fund

4. **Equity Income Funds:** These funds seek high current yield by investing primarily in equity securities which pay dividends, REITs, utilities, and financial stocks are usually highly represented in these funds. Speculative, high-risk stocks should not be in an equity income fund.

  - **Suitable for:** Conservative investors who want high current yield. Capital appreciation should not be a high priority for investors in these funds.
  - **Examples:** T. Rowe Price Equity Income Fund, Vanguard Equity Income Fund, Fidelity Equity Income Fund

5. **Specialty/Sector Funds:** These funds invest in securities of a specific industry or sector of the economy such as health care, technology, leisure, utilities, or precious metals. By investing primarily in one sector, they do not offer the element of downside protection found in mutual funds that invest in a broad range of industries. The funds, however, do enable investors to diversify holdings among many companies within an industry, a safer approach than investing directly in one particular company.

   - **Suitable for:** Investors seeking to invest in a particular industry who can monitor industry performance regularly. Investors must be willing to assume the risk of potential loss in value of their investment in the hope of achieving large gains. They are not suitable for investors who must protect their principal.
   - **Examples:** Fidelity Select Biotechnology Fund, TIAA CREF Real Estate Securities, T. Rowe Price Science & Technology Fund

6. **International/Global Funds:** International funds seek growth through investment in stocks from companies abroad, while global funds seek growth from equities around the world including the United States. They provide a way to diversify your mutual fund portfolio because foreign markets do not always move in tandem with the U.S. market.

   - **Suitable for:** Investors who are willing to accept a high degree of risk for the potential of high capital appreciation. In isolation, most funds that have foreign stocks are considered more risky than domestic funds. They are not suitable for investors who must conserve capital or maximize potential income.
   - **Examples:** Fidelity China Region Fund, TIAA CREF International Equity Fund, Vanguard International Growth Fund

Bond Mutual Funds

Bond funds make up about 40% of all funds, with more than $2 trillion invested in them. Like equity mutual funds, you have a lot of choice with fixed income funds. Active and passive bond funds are available as well as funds that invest in all the major types of fixed income securities such as Treasuries, corporates, and municipals. Although there are multisector bond funds that invest in a wide variety of different bond types, most bond funds distinguish themselves by the specific segment of the bond market they invest in. Most pay income on a monthly basis, which can be reinvested or distributed.

Prices of bonds tend to move inversely with changes in interest rates. Typically, a rise in rates will adversely affect bond prices and, accordingly, a fund's share price. The longer a fund's maturity and duration, the more its share price is likely to react to interest rates.

The main advantage of bond mutual funds over owning individual bonds is the low-cost diversification and professional management they provide. Bond mutual funds are managed by experienced financial professionals who decide which issues to purchase or sell. Bond mutual funds hold issues from across many industries or governments, which reduces the credit risk taken. The default or bad performance of a few bonds in a portfolio can be offset by the many other fixed income securities in the fund. A bond mutual fund is also more liquid than individual debt issues and generally requires a smaller initial investment.

The main disadvantage of bond mutual funds is that there is no guarantee that you will get the amount invested in the fund back in the future. There is no set final maturity date and coupon rate in a bond mutual fund. They are not geared for investors who need a specific dollar amount in the future from their investment or a certain income stream going forward. To help potential investors evaluate their holdings, most fixed income mutual funds give the average credit quality, maturity, and duration of their portfolio at a recent snapshot point in time, along with their past performance.

Money Market Mutual Funds

Money market funds offer low absolute returns with minimal risk. These funds invest in cash, cash equivalents, and other safe short-term instruments and usually maintain a constant $1 share price. You should be aware that although these funds are very safe and liquid, they are not guaranteed by the U.S. government or the FDIC. Since the differences in yields are very small among money market mutual funds, it is important to keep a keen eye on the expense ratios of different offerings.

Some of these funds provide income that is tax-free from federal and state governments. As individual securities, such money market instruments generally have large purchase requirements, disqualifying the majority of individual investors from buying them. An attraction of money market funds is that they have substantially lower initial investment requirements, which are sometimes even lower than average mutual funds minimum requirements. Money market funds provide tremendous liquidity and capital preservation benefits. A negative aspect of these funds is that when the stock and bond markets are performing well, they can be a drag on the portfolios overall performance.

Balanced Mutual Funds

Balanced mutual funds combine stocks, bonds, and money market instruments in a single portfolio. These funds seek high total return through a combination of capital appreciation and current income. Some balanced funds try to keep their equity/fixed income/cash split at certain percentages. Others make active bets, overweighting certain asset classes based on relative valuation and their perceived economic outlook.

A new wave of balanced funds has hit the marketplace recently called *asset allocation* and *life cycle funds*. With names such as the XYZ Target 2030 Fund or the XYZ Retirement 2025 Fund, these funds are geared to people who need a certain amount of money on a specific date and want someone else to handle their asset allocation. They are a one-stop option for investors who seek a diversified portfolio in terms of specific assets, as well as different asset classes. Generally, in the early years of the funds, they are more heavily weighted in stocks, and as the target date approaches they become more conservative, raising significantly their weights in low-risk bonds and cash instruments. The aim of these funds is to get capital appreciation early on and preserve it for when the money is going to be needed. It is important to have confidence in the fund family providing the fund because nearly all life cycle products are "fund of funds," investing in a pool of mutual funds run under the same roof. If the mutual funds of the fund company are poor, the life cycle funds offered by them will be stinkers as well.

Life cycle funds invest your money based on your risk tolerance. Ranging from very conservative to aggressive mixes, these funds invest in a fairly static mix of stocks, bonds, and cash. With these mutual funds it is up to the investor to switch from one to the next as their circumstances change.

What to Look for in Choosing a Mutual Fund

People often focus too much on mutual fund performance when they are choosing a mutual fund. Many people buy "hot" funds which recently provided superior returns. Funds that are hot one year are often dogs the next year. If you use past performance as a criterion, make sure the metric that you stress is good long term consistent performance. You want to see how the fund did in bull and bear markets. A 5-year track record is the minimum you should want a fund to have before using performance as criterion in selecting a mutual fund. A good long term performance record for a portfolio manager is more likely to be due to skill than luck.

No one knows what the future will bring for a mutual fund. When choosing a fund, you should focus on qualities that are more quantifiable going forward. Expenses, risk, and manager tenure are three factors that every potential mutual fund buyer should investigate. Simply stated, you want to understand what the expenses, including the fund's tax efficiency, are. High costs take a big bite from what is ultimately returned to you. You want to know the risk level of the fund. How closely it tracks its benchmark and what is its historical volatility? Lastly, you should ascertain how long the portfolio manager has been managing the fund. You do not want to purchase a fund based on a prior manager's track record.

Remember, do your homework before placing money in any mutual fund. Understand the risk and reward potential for the fund. Know where it fits into your overall portfolio strategy and be mindful of the cost.

Exchange-Traded Funds

The investment product that has seen the greatest percentage growth in assets recently is exchange-traded funds (ETFs). At the end of 2005, assets held in ETFs exceeded $310 billion, a 207% increase since 2002. A recent Morgan Stanley report predicts the amount of money invested in ETFs will top $2 trillion in 2011.

Originally, you could buy ETFs linked only to the main indexes like the S&P 500 and the Nasdaq Composite. Over the past few years, the breadth of exchange-traded funds has expanded. In 2005 alone, the American Stock Exchange listed 46 new funds—a record number of listings for one year. In 2006, more than 50 new funds were added.

The new funds that have been created allow you to buy specialized sector and country portfolios. ETFs combine traits of individual and pooled securities. They are a package of securities rolled up into one security that is traded like a stock throughout the day on one of the major exchanges. See Figure 3.2 for examples of sector funds and proxies for large cap, mid cap, and small cap stocks.

Compared to individual securities and mutual funds, exchange-traded funds have many advantages. The main advantage of ETFs compared to individual securities is the diversification they provide. By holding several securities, ETFs are not subject to single security risk as individual securities obviously are. Check the constituents of any fund you are considering buying because there are some ETFs that are highly concentrated.

Most exchange-traded funds have lower costs than both active and passive mutual funds because they do not have to be concerned with investing inflows or raising cash for outflows. The expense ratios for ETFs are slightly lower than for indexed mutual funds and much lower

Figure 3.2 ETF Sector Funds and Major Benchmarks for Large Cap, Mid Cap, and Small Cap Stocks

Sector	ETF	Symbol
Consumer discretionary	S&P Select Consumer Discretionary SPDR	XLY
Consumer staples	S&P Select Consumer Staples SPDR	XLP
Energy	S&P Select Energy SPDR	XLE
Financials	S&P Select Financials SPDR	XLF
Health care	S&P Select Health Care SPDR	XLV
Industrials	S&P Select Industrials SPDR	XLI
Information technology	S&P Select Information Technology SPDR	XLK
Materials	S&P Select Materials SPDR	XLB
Telecommunication services	i Shares Dow Jones U.S. Telecom	IYZ
Utilities	S&P Select Utilities SPDR	XLU
Large cap	S&P 500	SPY
Mid cap	S&P Mid Cap 400	MDY
Small cap	i Shares S&P Small Cap 600	IJR

than for actively managed mutual funds. For example, the S&P 500 iShares ETF (IVV) has an expense ratio of only 0.09% versus 0.18% for the Vanguard 500 Index fund, one of the lowest cost offerings in the mutual fund industry. Also, their low turnover helps them to be much more tax-efficient than active mutual funds.

A major strength of ETFs is their transparency. Unlike active mutual funds, it is easy to decipher what securities make up an ETF at any moment. Mutual fund companies are reluctant to tell clients what the holdings in their funds are on a day-to-day basis.

ETFs trade throughout the day like stocks; they are not just priced at the close of the trading day like mutual funds. There is no minimum amount to set up and maintain in an exchange-traded fund; most money management companies require at least $2,500 to purchase a mutual fund. Unlike mutual funds, traders can short (borrow and buy back at a later date) and place limit orders (have some control of the price they receive when they trade) on ETFs. If mutual funds were as transparent as ETFs and were priced continuously throughout the day, their late-trading and market-timing transgressions would most likely never have occurred. Incidentally, to date there have been no enforcement actions taken by the SEC or any attorney general against any financial firms regarding ETFs.

ETFs do have some disadvantages compared to mutual funds. There are currently no active ETFs where you can hopefully get out-sized returns because of the abilities of a talented portfolio manager. Although the choices are expanding, there is still a limited selection of ETFs compared to mutual funds. The pickings are especially paltry with fixed income funds. At the end of November 2006 just 6 of the 333 ETFs listed on U.S. exchanges tracked bond indexes, according to the Investment Company Institute. Currently, no balanced ETFs are available that combine equity, fixed income, and cash instruments.

Most equity ETFs are still trying only to match an index or focus on a specific sector such as information technology. Since ETFs are relatively new products, they do not have long periods of performance history. Lastly, they are not cost effective for those who like to invest a set amount each month (dollar cost average) because in order to buy them you have to pay broker commissions for each trade. ETFs are cheap to own, but trading them can turn out to be expensive.

From an asset allocation vantage point, most people should keep the vast majority of their investment portfolio in mutual funds and/or exchange-traded funds. Low-cost diversified equity, fixed income, and money market funds should be the core of your invested assets. If you want to reduce the number of funds you own, balanced funds are an acceptable alternative. Other investments, including individual securities, should be supplements to low-cost funds. If you own individual securities, no single security should make up more than 10% of your portfolio.

Investments that pool securities offer diversification; in the case of active mutual funds, they also offer professional portfolio management. You are able to reduce your paperwork and keep tabs of your accounts by using mutual funds and exchange-traded funds. With pooled investments, it is important to buy funds with reasonable expenses. Fortunately, there are plenty of both passively and actively managed funds that have low costs and the possibility for strong returns.

Points to Remember

- The wrapping that an investment product comes in can make the difference between whether it is right or wrong for you.
- Individual securities offer higher return potential, but with higher risk than diversified investments.
- Derivative products come with leverage. While a little money down can reap substantial gains, you must be able to stomach the higher risk you take.
- Mutual funds provide professionally managed, diversified portfolios at a reasonable cost.
- Before you buy a mutual fund, look at the long term performance, risk, manager tenure, and cost.
- Exchange-traded funds trade like individual stocks and offer diversification, lower costs, tax efficiency, and transparency.
- Exchange-traded funds are not suitable for dollar cost averaging.
- Most people should keep the majority of their portfolio in low-cost mutual and exchange-traded funds.

CHAPTER 4

THE LOCATION OF YOUR ASSETS

CHOOSING THE RIGHT ACCOUNTS

You got to be careful if you don't know where you're going, because you might not get there.

YOGI BERRA

Where is your money located? Is it in a checking account? In a brokerage account? You have different account choices for the location of your money. By organizing your assets in the right types of accounts, you can keep more of your investment return. Separate accounts also help you earmark certain investments for specific purposes. This will help you keep your eye on your goal and make it easier for you to recognize the sacrifices needed to get there.

Most individual investment accounts are divided by their tax status: taxable, tax-deferred, and nontaxable. The holdings in taxable accounts are subject to taxes. In a tax-deferred account, taxes are levied at a later date. In a nontaxable account, taxes are never incurred. There are certain assets that are appropriate for a taxable account that are completely inappropriate for a nontaxable account and vice versa. For example, municipal bonds, which are not subject to federal and state taxes, may be right for some individuals to hold in a taxable account, but these bonds are totally inappropriate in a nontaxable account.

Nontaxable and tax-deferred accounts usually are set up with an important, long term goal in mind. Examples include 401(k) plans for retirement and 529 plans for a child's education. Taxable accounts are usually used for achieving a wide range of goals, such as saving for down payments for a home and car, increasing your capital base, and paying for a Caribbean vacation. The following lists will help you identify the securities that are more appropriate for taxable and tax-advantaged accounts:

- **Securities for Taxable Accounts**
    - Indexed mutual funds
    - Indexed exchange-traded funds
    - Municipal bonds
    - Stocks you plan to hold for more than a year
    - Tax-managed mutual funds

- **Securities for Tax-Advantaged Accounts**
    - Actively managed stock mutual funds
    - Real estate investment trusts (REITs)
    - Treasury Inflation-Protected Securities (TIPS)
    - High-yielding junk bonds
    - Stocks you plan to hold less than a year
    - Corporate bonds

Taxable Accounts

Taxes on investments have been lowered in recent years. The top tax rate for the majority of long term capital gains now is 15%, down from 20%. Also, dividends used to be taxed as ordinary income; now they are frequently taxed at just 15%.

Taxable accounts include traditional brokerage, checking, and savings accounts. Any realized capital gains and income earned are taxed in these accounts in the year that they occur. *Tax considerations should never be the sole factor and outweigh your investment analysis in determining what to buy, sell, or hold.* If you think one of your securities is about to have a sharp price decline, do not decide to take no action because of the tax consequences of the trade. That being said with all things being equal, holders of traditional accounts should try to make investment decisions that do not burden them with tremendous tax bills.

In taxable accounts you should try to include the most tax efficient investments. Index funds and tax-managed funds, in the form of mutual funds and ETFs, should comprise a big part of your equity position. These accounts have low turnover, low expenses, and additionally the tax-managed accounts actively try to minimize their taxable gains and income for their shareholders. Small cap index funds tend to have greater turnover and tax consequences than large cap index funds because stocks must be sold when they grow out of their small cap status and into the mid cap range.

International stocks and funds are also good candidates for a taxable account. Investors in international securities who pay foreign taxes can get a tax credit, but that credit is lost if the foreign equities are held in a tax-deferred account.

If you invest in individual stocks, you should try to hold your stocks for more than 1 year. You will then not have to pay short term capital gains taxes, which can range from 35% to 15%. A negative aspect of successful actively traded accounts is that they will pile up capital gains. If you happen to have more losses than gains, you can use up to $3,000 of losses to offset income from sources such as salary and trading gains. Excess losses can be carried over to offset gains in future years.

If you realize any short term losses in the current year, they must first be used to offset any short term gains you have that would otherwise be taxed at the higher ordinary income tax rate. Any extra short term losses can then be used to offset long term gains, which would otherwise be taxed at a lower rate. If you had the benefit of hindsight, you would put your investments that decline in value in the taxable accounts where at least you can benefit by offsetting some of your gains.

Your tax bracket helps determine the type of bonds that are most appropriate for your taxable accounts. Individuals in high tax brackets and high tax states should buy municipal bonds while ones in lower tax brackets should buy Treasuries and corporate bonds. Here is an easy formula to help you determine if a municipal bond is appropriate for inclusion in your portfolio:

$$\frac{\textbf{Tax-exempt yield}}{(\textbf{100\% -- your marginal tax rate})} = \textbf{taxable-equivalent yield}$$

If the tax-exempt yield is greater than the tax-equivalent yield, the muni would be appropriate to put in your taxable account. Here is an example for someone in the 28% tax bracket who is considering a municipal bond yielding 6%:

$$\frac{0.06}{(1 - 0.28)} = 8.33$$

The investor must get an 8.33% taxable yield to equal the 6% tax-free yield.

Liquidity should be stressed for the cash instruments used in a taxable account. Cash or other short term instruments like checking accounts are needed for everyday transactions. Since there is a likelihood that the cash position will need to be turned into "actual" cash, it is important that it is readily available to you. A portion of the cash position needs to be very liquid. You can seek higher yields in the cash position if you already have enough liquidity.

Tax-Advantaged Accounts

Tax-advantaged accounts fall into two categories:

1. Accounts that defer taxes until some point in the future
2. Accounts that are funded with after-tax dollars so that account owners do not have to pay taxes on the capital appreciation and income going forward

Investments in these tax-advantaged accounts compound more quickly than those in taxable accounts because they are not burdened with the bite that taxes take out of the principal year after year.

If you plan on being an active trader with part of your money, use a tax-advantaged account so you can delay or even avoid paying capital gains taxes. These types of accounts are also a better place to put your active, high-turnover mutual fund accounts.

Most tax-advantaged accounts are geared to a long term objective such as funding your retirement or your child's college education. High-yielding securities such as most fixed income securities and real estate investment trusts are better off in a tax-advantaged account.

Despite the recent tax law changes involving dividends, REITs are still taxed at the higher ordinary income rate. The new dividend tax law was intended to reduce the double taxation of dividends. REITs, however, since they are required by law to distribute at least 90% of their taxable income to investors, do not pay corporate taxes on that income. That means income from REITs is still taxed at ordinary income rates, which can be as high as 35%.

It is also better to hold TIPS (Treasury Inflation-Protected Securities) in a tax-advantaged account. All the annual interest payments of TIPS are taxed as ordinary income, even though you do not receive any inflation-adjusted additions to your principal (imputed interest) until the bond is redeemed.

Retirement Accounts

One of the main goals of many is to be able to retire comfortably without having to fear that their assets will run out. People often underestimate the amount of money they will need in order to maintain their lifestyle after they stop working. Many financial experts believe that you will need at least 85% of your preretirement income just to maintain your preretirement lifestyle. Advances in medicine are allowing people to live longer, which would require them to have large nest eggs to spread over their retirement years. The majority of men and women who reach the age of 65 will live into their 80s or beyond. According to the National Center for Health Statistics, by 2050, there will be about a million Americans at least 100 years old. It is conceivable that retirement in some cases will last over 40 years.

Retirees' health care costs are substantial. Even though Medicare insures them, people older than age 65 spend more than twice as much on medical care from their own wallets as the average American. Medicare doesn't cover such costs as nursing home care, and Medicare beneficiaries still have annual deductions and coinsurance payments. According to Watson Wyatt Worldwide, in 2005 retirees 65 and older spent on average $5,150 on medical care, including premiums and out-of-pocket costs.

Going forward, the traditional sources of retirement income, social security and pensions, will likely make up a smaller fraction of the assets people will be getting when they stop working. These traditional sources of funds will need to be supplemented with other sources of capital.

Fortunately, there are other tax-advantaged retirement accounts available to individuals. Individuals though need the wherewithal to take advantage of these vehicles and to start at a young age. The earlier you start, the more you can let the power of compounding work for you. It also allows you to be more aggressive with your security picks in the early years when you know the money will not be needed for a long period of time.

Employer-Sponsored Plans

Most large employers offer their workers 401(k), 403(b), or a similar type of retirement account. Unfortunately, many people do not take advantage of these plans. Studies show that 26% of eligible workers do not contribute to an employer-sponsored plan and only 8% contribute the maximum allowed. More than half of today's 55-year-olds have less than $50,000 in their defined-contribution plans, according to research from McKinsey & Company.

Putting money in your employers plan has several benefits. First, your investments grow tax-deferred in these accounts. By delaying the tax bill, more of your money is working for you over the years. In essence, the government is subsidizing your retirement savings by deferring income tax on the amount you save.

Contributing to these accounts lowers the amount of taxable income you have on your yearly tax form, lowering the taxes you pay to the government annually. For every $1 you contribute to your account, your pay may be decreased by only 60 or 70 cents. These plans also allow you to contribute larger amounts than other retirement vehicles. In 2006, you were able to contribute as much as $15,000 to a 401(k) plan.

Employer-sponsored retirement plans are extremely convenient and instill some discipline in the investment process. The money is taken directly out of your paycheck. You do not have to mail in a check every week or go to a branch to contribute to the account. By never getting your hands on the money, you will not be tempted to spend it on something you probably do not need. It provides a great mechanism for forced savings. Also, by investing regularly you are engaging in dollar cost averaging—buying more shares of the funds at low absolute prices and less at high absolute prices which should over time reduce your risk. It will prevent you from buying a lot of shares at the top of the market and selling out at the bottom. Diversifying over time, by not investing all at once will in more cases than not be a plus for your portfolio.

Another feature that is great for keeping with your investment plan is that many 401(k) plans offer an automatic rebalance feature. If requested, a few times during the year your funds will be rebalanced to your desired weights. This allows you to maintain your initial asset allocation, without having to buy and sell funds yourself. If your circumstances or the investment outlook change, you always have the option of changing your mix of funds.

The icing on the cake for why 401(k)s should be used by workers is that in many cases employers match some of your contributions. At the very least you should contribute enough to get the company match. *It is free money.* In some situations, an employee has to stay with a company for a specific period of time before the matching contribution will "vest" and really become the property of the employee. Companies that match usually do so for an amount that is between 3% and 6% of the employee's yearly contributions.

A negative of employer-sponsored plans is that in many cases the choices are pretty limited. Rank-and-file employees have virtually no say in the investment choices offered. Many plans just have a few equity and fixed income funds and in a lot of cases their quality is mediocre, at best. Some have been adding balanced funds which have tilts toward investment styles such as aggressive growth, growth and income, or capital preservation. Hopefully in the future, companies will offer their employees a wider variety of choices in their retirement plans.

If you switch jobs, it is imperative to transfer your 401(k) plan into an individual retirement account (IRA) or your new employer's plan. You should not cash out of the plan and spend the assets you have built up. A voluntary job change should not interrupt your retirement savings. By transferring your plan into another retirement vehicle, you will avoid taxes and penalties, keep your assets tax-advantaged, and continue to have your money benefit from the power of compounding.

Should Your Company's Stock Be in Your Retirement Plan?

Many public companies give you the option to own the company stock in their plan. According to Hewitt Associates, for plans that offer company stock, about one in four employees have half or more of their 401(k) balance invested in it.

Regardless of their opinion of their company's prospects, employees should not put a large percentage of their retirement plan in their company's stock. I would argue that no more than 10% of the employee's holdings should be in the company's stock. Employees should diversify their risks. By working there, an employee already has a large exposure to the company. Many people get their health coverage and other benefits through their employer. If tough times besiege the company, employees who hold a large percentage of the company stock can get hit with the double whammy of a large stock decline and a job loss. Talk to any of the former employees of Enron or WorldCom if you do not think this can happen to you.

Keogh Plans

For people who are self-employed, Keogh plans, or H.R. 10 plans, are available as a retirement option. A Keogh plan is simply a qualified retirement plan for businesses that are not incorporated. The plans were named after Eugene Keogh, a congressman from Brooklyn, N.Y., who sponsored the legislation that created the program in 1962.

Everyone who has a Keogh account is entitled to tax deferments on the capital gains, interest, and dividends generated until funds are withdrawn, usually following retirement (when taxpayers may be in a substantially lower tax bracket). Participants in Keogh plans are subject to the same restrictions on distributions as IRAs: namely, that they cannot be made without penalty before age 59½ and distributions must begin before age 70½.

The most attractive feature of Keoghs is that the contribution levels are much more liberal than other retirement vehicles. Like IRAs, a Keogh plan must be established by the end of the year but contributions can be made at any time up until April 15 of the next year. The maximum annual contribution to a Keogh depends on whether it is a defined contribution or a defined benefit plan.

For 2006, the annual benefit for a defined benefit plan participant cannot be greater than a participant's average compensation for their highest three consecutive years or $175,000. If it is a defined contribution plan, annual contributions and other additions in 2005 (except for earnings) cannot exceed the lesser of 100% of the compensation actually paid to the participant or $44,000. If you have employees and open a Keogh for yourself, you must offer a Keogh plan to your workers and contribute to their accounts as well. These contributions, however, are deductible and can go toward reducing the cost of your overall contribution.

If you have self-employment income, you can contribute to a Keogh plan only if you are making a profit. This means that until your business is making a profit, you will not be able to make contributions. Another negative aspect of these plans is that they require more paperwork than other retirement vehicles. They are subject to many difficult administration and operating rules. In almost all cases, you should use a third-party administrator to help you stay within the compliance requirements.

Traditional Individual Retirement Accounts

The most popular retirement vehicle is the traditional individual retirement account (IRA). These accounts are available to virtually everyone who works, is married to someone who is employed, and/or receives taxable alimony. There are no income restrictions on them to be eligible. Unlike some other retirement accounts, in which you have a fixed menu of choices, your investment options for an IRA are virtually limitless. Mutual funds, individual stocks and bonds, certificates of deposit, and exchange-traded funds can all be purchased in an IRA.

You can contribute up to $4,000 a year to an IRA when you file your taxes singly and $8,000 when you are married and file jointly. Workers over age 50 can contribute even more; they can make additional "catch-up" contributions of $1,000 a year. See Figure 4.1.

Contributions to these accounts are tax-deductible (depending on income level) and allow investments to compound tax-free for a long

Figure 4.1 Maximum IRA Contributions

Tax Year	Single Filing Status	
	Up to Age 50	Older than Age 50
2006–2007	$4,000	$5,000
2008 and later	$5,000	$6,000

period of time. Taxes are paid on the earnings when they are withdrawn from the IRA. With a traditional IRA, withdrawals must begin by age 70½ and funds can be withdrawn without penalty at age 59½. In addition to being subject to income taxes, funds withdrawn before age 59½ are subject to a 10% early withdrawal penalty on the earnings. There are some exceptions to paying the 10% penalty, such as withdrawing the money for a first-time home purchase, qualified education expenses, and if the account holder passes away resulting in a payout to a beneficiary.

Roth IRA

A new type of retirement account is the Roth IRA. Named after Senator William Roth of Delaware, Roth IRAs have some major distinctions from traditional IRAs. In a Roth IRA contributions are never tax-deductible, but withdrawals during retirement are tax-free. You can even continue contributing to a Roth past age 70½. Unlike traditional IRAs, where you have to begin taking distributions at age 70½, with Roth IRAs you never have to take withdrawals. This flexibility makes Roth IRAs better for estate planning than traditional IRAs. With a Roth you are not going to burden your heirs with a tax bill.

Like traditional IRAs, the Roth IRA allows you to choose from a wide variety of investments. The contribution levels allowed for the two types of individual retirement accounts are the same but the eligibility requirements are more stringent with a Roth. Single filers can only have income up to $110,000 and joint filers can only have income up to $160,000 to be able to contribute the full amount and get all the tax benefits of a Roth IRA. The principal balance in the Roth can be withdrawn tax-free anytime. No taxes are paid on earnings provided the account has been established for at least 5 years. Earnings, though, are subject to a 10% tax penalty for early withdrawal. The same exceptions to paying the 10% penalty that apply to the traditional IRA can be applied to the Roth IRA.

Traditional IRA versus Roth IRA

Which type of IRA is better for you, a traditional or a Roth IRA? It depends. Your income level may make the decision for you. As stated previously, single filers with income over $110,000 and joint filers with income over $160,000 cannot contribute to a Roth IRA.

If you qualify for a Roth IRA, the traditional IRA may be preferable if you think your tax bracket in retirement will be significantly lower than it is when you are making contributions to the retirement plan. If you plan to be very conservative with your retirement investment account, a traditional IRA may make more sense since the lower risk will translate into a low absolute return and thus lower taxes to be taken out during retirement. If someone cannot afford to part with the tax taken out during the Roth contribution, a traditional IRA is often the option chosen. This is a weak argument for not having a Roth, but it is one of the major reasons people who qualify choose traditional over Roth IRAs. People focus on the short term cost, not the long term benefits. See Figure 4.2.

In the majority of situations, the Roth IRA is the better choice. The focus on your retirement account should not be what is best for you in the present, but what is best for you the date you actually retire. It is important to think in the long term for retirement decisions. Withdrawing money 100% tax-free in retirement but taking taxes out when you contribute to the plan in a Roth is generally better than choosing a traditional IRA, where you put in pretax dollars and get a deduction but have taxes taken out in retirement. What do you want—periodic short term pain or major long term pain? You are better off with the periodic short term pain. It is analogous to deciding whether you would rather change your oil in your car every 3,000 miles or put a new engine in your car every 4 years.

You are better off in a Roth if you expect to be in a higher tax bracket in retirement. Roths also provide more money if your tax rate stays the same because you earn a tax-advantaged return on more dollars than you would with a traditional IRA. Additionally, Roth IRAs gives you much more flexibility. You are never forced to make withdrawals with a Roth. You can withdraw the money on your terms, not someone else's.

See Figure 4.3 for a comparison of how much money you would accumulate in a Roth IRA versus a traditional IRA in various scenarios. An annual contribution of $2,000 and the retirement age of 65 are constants in each scenario. In the majority of situations you end up with more money in a Roth. The scenarios in which the traditional IRA works out to be the better choice are when the future federal income tax rate drops substantially from the contributor's earlier rate.

Figure 4.2 Comparison of Traditional and Roth IRAs

	Traditional IRA	Roth IRA
Tax Status of Earnings	Earnings are taxed as regular income based on your income level at time of withdrawal	No taxes are paid on earnings provided that account has been open for 5 years and at least one of the following applies: • Age 59½ or older • First home purchases ($10,000 limit) • Death or disability
Distribution Status	Must start by age 70½	No mandatory distribution requirement
10% Early Withdrawal Penalty Waived for	Postsecondary education expenses First home purchases ($10,000 limit) Death or disability Certain medical expenses Satisfaction of certain IRS tax liens	Postsecondary education expenses First home purchases ($10,000 limit) Death or disability Certain medical expenses Satisfaction of certain IRS tax liens
Rollovers and Transfers	Allowed to and from other IRAs and employer plans	Traditional IRA to Roth rollover only allowed for individuals with less than $100,000 modified adjusted gross income

Figure 4.3 Comparison of Roth and Traditional IRA Returns

Input Assumptions									
Annual contribution	$2,000	$2,000	$2,000	$2,000	$2,000	$2,000	$2,000	$2,000	$2,000
Contribution years	30	30	10	30	30	40	40	40	10
Assumed rate of return	5%	5%	5%	10%	5%	5%	10%	10%	10%
Current Federal income tax rate	25%	35%	25%	25%	28%	35%	35%	28%	25%
Future Federal income tax rate	25%	15%	25%	25%	25%	25%	10%	28%	25%
Retirement age	65	65	65	65	65	65	65	65	65
Total After-Tax Distribution									
Roth IRA	$139,522	$139,522	$26,414	$361,887	$139,522	$253,680	$973,704	$973,704	$35,062
Traditional IRA	$132,550	$154,405	$25,967	$326,992	$135,088	$247,951	$1,007,267	$827,266	$33,901

A law passed in May 2006 that goes into affect in 2010 provides individuals with high incomes a backdoor way to start putting money into a Roth. Currently, anyone who makes more than $100,000 is restricted from converting a traditional IRA to a Roth. In 2010, you will be able to convert whatever money you've accumulated in your traditional IRA into a Roth. You will be able to in effect skirt the income limitations of a Roth and convert it year after year from a traditional IRA. A negative of this new law is that when you convert to a Roth, regardless of whether it's a nondeductible IRA or not, you must calculate the tax due for the conversion based on all the money you have in all IRA accounts you own. For example, if you have $100,000 in total IRA assets and $20,000 of that came from nondeductible IRA contributions, then 20% of the amount you convert would not be taxed while 80% would be ($80,000 divided by $100,000).

Whether you choose a Roth or traditional IRA, it is important to fund it as early as possible in the year. Do not wait until the last minute on April 15 to make your contribution. By funding it early you give your money more time to compound. If you wait until the tax deadline to fund your IRA each year, you miss out on 16½ months of potential tax-deferred growth. More importantly, you avoid the possibility of passing up funding your retirement account to cover some other expense that props up at the time. Let's face it—the contribution to your retirement account is not the most exciting expenditure you can make; it is, however, probably the most rewarding in the long run. See Figure 4.4.

You are doing yourself a great service by setting up a retirement account. Having this money segregated from your other accounts makes it less likely that you will be tempted to tap into it before your retirement

Figure 4.4 Comparison of IRA Returns According to When Made in Tax Year*

IRA Beginning Age	Total Years Investing	Contributions at Beginning of Each Year	Contributions at Tax Deadline
35	30	$539,540	$494,566
45	20	$244,990	$224,626
55	10	$85,974	$78,895

*Assumes a 7% annual rate of return and the maximum contribution according to IRS regulations.

years and lose the benefit of long term compounding. Investment accounts with a clear life-goal objective makes your overall financial planning a little easier.

Some of the decisions about which retirement accounts you are eligible for are determined by your income and work status. For example, if a single filer's income is above $110,000, he cannot contribute to a Roth IRA; if a person is self-employed, she obviously cannot contribute to a 401(k) plan. If you are employed at a company that offers a 401(k) or similar type retirement plan and the company matches part of your contribution, your employers plan should be the first one you fund. The free money of the company match is one of the best financial deals available. At a minimum, you should contribute the percentage from your paycheck that gets you the match.

Money in a Roth grows not just tax-deferred, but tax-free. By having a Roth with another tax-deferred retirement account you get some tax diversification. If your tax rate during retirement is high, the Roth IRA will be beneficial; if your tax rate during retirement is low, a tax-deferred account would be advantageous. Tax-free withdrawals, the gamut of investment choices, along with the flexibility of taking out the money when you want, make the Roth the choice to fund after you get the match from your employer's plan. If you do not qualify for a Roth, a traditional IRA is still a solid option for your retirement savings. Tax-deferred growth plus a deduction on your taxes is a pretty good combination.

Investment Accounts for Education

Most parents dream of sending their children to college. Besides the academic and social benefits of going to college, higher education tends to translate into a lot more dollars earned. On average, college graduates make a million dollars more over their lifetime than high school graduates make (see Figure 4.5). And for many desirable entry-level jobs, a college degree is required for employment.

Unfortunately, the cost of a college education is staggering and continues to outpace inflation year in and year out. According to the College Board, in 2005–2006 the average undergraduate 4-year private college tuition was $21,235 per year and the average 4-year public

Figure 4.5 Correlation between Education and Salary

Highest Educational Level	Medium Annual Salary
Less than high school	$21,645
High school	$30,766
Bachelor's degree	$49,886

Source: Bureau of Labor Statistics of the U.S. Department of Labor, 2004.

college tuition was $5,491 a year. See Figure 4.6. When you factor in room and board and other essential expenses, many private schools cost more than $40,000 a year. What will be the price tag if your child also wants to go to graduate school?

For the majority of people, these types of costs can translate into massive student loans that can take years to pay off. According to the Department of Education's National Center for Education Statistics, about 65% of students who graduated in the 2003–2004 school year did so after getting student loans. For college students who took out a loan, the average debt was $19,202. For medical students the debt load is much higher. A recent study by the Association of American Medical Colleges shows that the average medical student graduates with nearly $100,000 in student loan debt.

Full academic and athletic scholarships do exist. Unfortunately, the chances of a child receiving a full scholarship are very small. It would certainly be nice for your child to receive a full ride, but you should not expect that he or she will, and definitely do not financially plan for that.

Figure 4.6 Private College Tuition

Institution	2006–2007 Tuition
George Washington University	$37,820
University of Richmond	$36,550
Sarah Lawrence	$36,088
Kenyon	$36,050
Vassar	$36,030
Bucknell	$36,002
Bennington	$35,250
Columbia University	$35,166
Wesleyan	$35,144
Trinity College	$35,130

Source: *The Chronicle of Higher Education.*

To help plan and pay for educational expenses, parents can set up certain specialized investment accounts that offer many benefits compared to traditional brokerage or savings accounts. As with retirement savings, earmarking a certain account toward a specific goal such as educational savings lowers the chance that this money will be used on the inevitable expenses that come up in daily life. Funding an educational account soon after a child is born is a very smart move. Starting early gives you more options and allows the power of compounding to work for a longer period of time. Equities should hold a prominent place in educational investment accounts because of their ability to outperform inflation over time. As the target date approaches for a child's freshman year, however, there should be a shift to more conservative investments such as high-quality bonds and money market instruments. You do not want the amount that has been accumulated in the account to be subject to a sharp decline, just before it is going to be needed for tuition payments. A discussion of the specialized savings accounts available follows.

529 Plans

Named from Section 529 of the Internal Revenue Code, 529 Plans were established to help families set aside and accumulate funds for future college costs. Like retirement accounts, 529 plans provide tax benefits that make them enticing to establish. Currently, every state has at least one 529 plan available. Be aware that these plans can be very different from state to state. This makes it imperative that you read the details of the plan before placing any money in it. Review the options carefully, paying close attention to participation and residency requirements, investment options, fees and expenses, and state tax treatment.

The 529 plans are usually categorized as either prepaid plans or savings plans with some having characteristics of both. The prepaid plans are similar to defined benefit plans, where you contribute an agreed amount in exchange for future benefits; savings plans are similar to defined contribution plans (examples include IRAs and 401(k) plans) where investors make investment decisions on their own. A *prepaid tuition plan* is a college savings plan that is guaranteed to rise in value at the same rate as college tuition. This allows parents to "lock in" current tuition rates. These programs are usually used for in-state public universities. Some states will provide a cash equivalent for use out-of-state, but some penalties may apply.

A *college savings plan* is a tax-deferred account used to pay for higher education expenses. There is no restriction on the amount of income a contributor can have to fund this type of plan. These programs offer more flexibility because they can be used for educational expenses in universities both in state and out of state. The full value of your 529 savings plan can be used at any accredited college in the country. Also, the account belongs to the parents, giving them control as to how the money is spent. For example, a child cannot decide to skip college and take the money saved for him in a 529 plan and spend it on a new car without getting his parents' consent.

Attractions of 529 Plans

If you open a 529 savings plan, you can sock away a lot of money, cut your taxes, and probably pick up a state tax break. Parents can easily transfer funds from one child to another with a 529 plan. The maximum total contributions vary by state and are inflation-adjusted, but in many cases they are in the $200,000 to $300,000 range. Couples can contribute up to $24,000 per year to a 529 savings account per child without triggering the gift tax. It is also permitted to "front load" 5 years of gifts in a single year, allowing an individual to put up to $55,000 into a 529 plan account at one time.

One of the major attractions of 529 plans is that in many states contributions can be deducted from income on the state tax return. Investors should check to see if their state plan has this tax benefit, which would provide an advantage compared to out-of-state plans. Furthermore, the capital appreciation and income from the investment in the plan accumulate tax-free when used for qualified education expenditures. This allows the capital gains and income earned to compound more than if taxes were taken out each year.

Disadvantages of 529 Plans

There are some negative characteristics of 529 plans. The investment choices in most plans are very limited. A few equity and fixed-income mutual funds are usually the only options in the plan. After selecting which portfolios to invest in, the contributor has no direct say in how the portfolios are managed. Another negative is that many 529 plans have high fees, especially when advisors sell them. Lastly, the law enabling tax-free withdrawals from a 529 account is set to expire in 2010. Unless, the law is extended, the earnings component of withdrawals will be taxable starting in 2011.

Coverdell Education Savings Accounts

Coverdell Education Savings Accounts (ESAs), previously known as Education IRAs, are another vehicle designed to help people save for educational costs. The Coverdell ESA is a custodial account or trust set up solely for the purpose of paying qualified expenses for the designated beneficiary of the account. According to the IRS, qualified educational expenses include tuition, fees, books, supplies, and equipment required for enrollment.

Advantages of Coverdell Education Savings Accounts

The main advantage of Coverdell ESAs over a 529 plans is that they offer a much wider range of investment options. With a 529 plan you can only choose the limited investments in the state's plan; however, with an ESA you can invest in any mutual fund, ETF, or individual stock and bond of your choosing. An ESA can also be used for elementary and secondary education, not just college and graduate school. Also with the Coverdell ESA, the tax-free status of these accounts will definitely continue after 2010.

Disadvantages of Coverdell Education Savings Accounts

Unfortunately, Coverdell ESAs have many disadvantages. Contributions may be made only until the beneficiary reaches age 18 and are limited to $2,000 per year. These maximum contribution levels make it difficult to fully fund future college tuition. The money in these accounts must be used by the time the child reaches age 30, or the earnings will be taxed as ordinary income and a 10% penalty is imposed. These age limits do not apply to beneficiaries with special needs. Furthermore, although earnings accumulate tax-free, contributions are not deductible on federal or state income tax. Also, Coverdell ESAs count as the beneficiary's asset, which can reduce the amount of financial aid a student is eligible for.

Saving for Retirement versus Saving for a Child's Education

Unfortunately, most people have limited financial resources. Choices have to be made; we cannot just buy everything we want. A tough decision many adults have to face is what percentage of their savings should go toward retirement and what percentage should go toward their children's education.

All things being equal, a higher percentage of your savings should go toward retirement. For the vast majority, retirement is for a longer period than is postsecondary education; moreover, retirement usually requires a greater yearly cost as compared to college or graduate school. Conventional wisdom says: you can borrow for your child's education but you cannot borrow for your retirement needs. There is no financial aid for retirement, but there is financial aid available for college.

Time is also on your side with loans for education. Parents and/or students have a long period of time to pay off student loans. Often, many loan providers are very liberal with payment terms and offer favorable interest rates. Once you reach your retirement years you have much less financial flexibility.

The pot you have to work with in retirement is: your retirement savings, any assets you acquired over the years including your home, a pension if you are eligible for one, and Social Security benefits. Money saved in retirement accounts can be spent on anything including helping your children with their education. On the other hand, a 529 plan or Coverdell ESA has to be spent on educational expenses. Lastly, your child who has a major vested interest in his or her education can help fund the educational account. Through part-time work, grants, and scholarships, students can help assume some of the responsibility of financing their college education.

Points to Remember

- By organizing your assets into the right type of accounts, you can keep more of your investment returns.
- Tax considerations should never determine investment decisions.
- A taxable account is the best place to deposit your individual stocks, index funds, tax-managed funds, international stocks, and stocks

you want to hold longer than a year. Active mutual funds and securities you want to hold less than a year are more appropriate in a tax-advantaged account.

- People in high tax brackets and in high tax states should buy municipal bonds, while people in lower tax brackets and lower tax states should buy Treasury and corporate bonds.
- At a minimum, employees should invest enough in their employer's retirement plan to get the company match.
- Regardless of your opinion of your company's stocks prospects, you should not put more than 10% of your retirement plan in the company stock.
- In the majority of situations, a Roth IRA is a better choice than a traditional IRA.
- The choice between a Roth and a traditional IRA boils down to flexibility and whether you want to pay tax now or later on your contributions.
- The capital appreciation and income from your investment in a 529 plan accumulates tax-free when you use it for qualified education expenses. In many states your contribution can be deducted from income on your state return.
- All things being equal, a higher percentage of your savings should go toward your retirement rather than your child's educational fund.

CHAPTER 5

THE COSTS OF FINANCIAL ASSETS

UNDERSTANDING THE IMPACT OF FEES AND TAXES

There's no free lunch.

MILTON FRIEDMAN

In the investment world, costs come in many forms. Some are overt like commissions on a mutual fund (called *loads*). Others are less obvious like the difference between the bid and ask price of a stock, called *the spread*. Before allocating a dime to an investment, you should understand what it costs to buy it and what the ongoing costs will be to own it. Your overall investment results can be vastly improved if you fully understand the costs.

In many cases the high-priced product or service is no better than the inexpensive one. In most cases, you would be better off buying the lower-cost investment vehicle. Remember: while *returns for most investments cannot be predicted, their costs can be predicted with a fair degree of certainty.* If you educate yourself as to the costs of the investment products and services available, you can save vast amounts on your expenses without sacrificing returns.

Brokerage Costs

Brokers are the main conduits that investors use to purchase and sell securities. Brokers charge a brokerage commission, which is the fee paid to a stockbroker by a client for the act of buying or selling shares of a corporation in the securities markets. The brokerage commission covers expenses for the broker such as transaction fees paid to the securities exchange, order-handling fees, and the time and effort in completing the trade. The combination of intense competition and technological advances has led to a sharp decline in brokerage costs over the past decade.

Discount versus Full-Service Brokers

In 1975, the government deregulated brokerage commissions. This action divided brokers into two groups: discount brokers and full-service brokers. Charles Schwab, one of the first discount brokers, was started right after deregulation.

Discount brokers offer low commissions with limited service. Most discount brokers charge less than $15 per trade when the trades are executed online. The lowest prices are usually reserved for investors who either have a lot of money with the firm or are very active traders. The customer support discount brokers provide is usually minimal. Their main clients are do-it-yourself investors who make their own financial decisions and do not want to pay a lot in transaction costs. If you are a knowledgeable investor or want to be Joe Day Trader, a discount brokerage is where you should have your investment account.

Full-service brokers charge high commissions and offer extensive handholding. They provide services for investors such as advice and research with "buy," "sell," and "hold" recommendations from analysts at their firm. A trade of 100 shares of a stock can generate a commission of $75 at a full-service firm. If you educate yourself, you would realize that the prices full-service brokers charge for executing trades are not worth it. Only novice investors, ones who need a very specialized service, and people who do not care about the price they are paying should even consider having a brokerage account with the Merrill Lynchs and Smith Barneys of this world.

In addition to the commission on market orders, many investment firms charge up to $5 more for limit orders. A *market order* is an order to buy or sell a stock at the current best available price. A *limit order*, on the other hand, is an order to buy or sell a stock for a specific price or better. The danger of a limit order from a broker perspective is that there is a chance that the trade will not be executed because of the price target not being reached. When this occurs the broker does not get a commission. With a market order, there is pretty much a guarantee that there will be someone at the other end willing to buy or sell your security at the market price and subsequently the broker getting his commission. Limit orders give you more control of the price you receive and can be very helpful in transactions involving small and illiquid stocks. For the extra cost (if it is even charged) using limit orders is a prudent tactic.

Another cost involved in transacting stocks is the bid/ask spread. The *bid price* is the price you can sell a stock for, and the *ask price* is the price at which you can buy the stock. The ask price is always a little higher than the bid price. The difference between the bid and ask price is the *spread.* This spread compensates the market maker, the middleman in the transaction on the exchange, who tries to match the buy and sell orders for the same security. Large cap stocks and stocks with fairly strong trading volumes have bid/ask spreads of less than 10 cents a share. Less liquid and lower-priced stocks have higher bid/ask spreads in percentage terms.

The bid/ask spread is intended to compensate the market makers and specialists for the risk they take in setting a market for a stock and keeping the market liquid. Overall, frequent traders are hampered the most by the bid/ask spread. It is another cost of doing business on top of broker commissions, which makes outperforming the market a difficult task.

The overriding goal for brokers is for their clients to keep a large amount of money with them and for their trades to be done with their firm. Besides costs associated with the trading of securities, there are other fees that brokerage firms sometimes charge to earn more revenue. You should check before signing up with a broker to see what fees apply. These nickel-and-dime charges are a big reason many customers get ticked off with the brokerage industry:

Inactivity fee: A charge that occurs if you do not execute enough trades in a certain time period. The lower the number of trades made, the lower the amount of revenue to the broker.

Transfer fees: Fees that are charged if you switch your account to another firm. ETrade charges $25 to $60 for moving assets to another firm. Charles Schwab charges $25 for a partial transfer out and $50 to move all your money.

Account maintenance fees: Fees that are levied when clients have special requests that extend the resources of the brokerage firm. Retrieving old financial documents, updating data in their customer files, and mailing costs for account statements and order confirmations are examples of events which can trigger these charges.

Minimum account balance fees: Like banks, some firms charge you a fee if you do not maintain a certain amount of money in your account. The more assets you have with a brokerage firm, the more money the broker can earn from you.

How to Invest without Brokers

Dividend reinvestment plans (DRIPs) provide a way to bypass brokers when buying stocks. These are programs that use cash dividends to purchase additional shares of stock. Many corporations allow you to buy the initial shares directly from them. In other cases, you only need to buy one share from a broker to participate in a DRIP.

Some companies offer DRIP participants the added benefit of reinvesting their dividends at a discount from the prevailing market price. DRIP plans are geared for long term investors in a stock. A disadvantage of these plans is that the participant has little control of the execution price in which the trades are made. To find out if a particular company offers a direct purchase plan, call the investor relations department or check on websites like www.net-stockdirect.com, www.equiserve.com, and www.directinvesting.com.

Some fixed income securities can also be bought without the use of a broker. The entire line of Treasuries, including Treasury bills, notes, bonds, Treasury Inflation-Protected Securities (TIPS), and Series I and EE savings bonds, can be purchased by individuals directly from the U.S. Treasury through Treasury Direct, which can be accessed on the Internet at www.treasurydirect.gov. If you do not have access to the Internet, you can get an application for the Treasury Direct program by contacting your nearest Federal Reserve Bank or the U.S. Department of Public Debt (800-722-2678).

There are no transaction or brokerage fees when you buy Treasuries through Treasury Direct. The minimum investments in Treasury Direct are $10,000 for Treasury bills, $5,000 for Treasury notes that mature in less than 5 years, and $1,000 for Treasury securities that mature in 5 years or more.

Mutual Fund Fees

When you buy mutual funds, there are certain costs that are avoidable and others that are inherent in the product. The best way to save the largest amount of money is to buy a mutual fund directly from a no-load mutual fund company. If you purchase the fund directly from the mutual fund company without using a broker or advisor, you will not have to pay a commission, called *a load*. If you purchase the fund through a broker or investment advisor, you probably will have to pay some type of load. The load can run up to 6.25% of the initial purchase value. For example, Putnam funds have a 5.25% front-end load on their A shares. Different types of funds have different charges to cover the cost of any of the advice you received in selecting the fund. Each share class for load funds has different sales charges and different fee structures. The basic definitions of the shares classes are:

- *A Shares* are sold with an initial (front-end) sales charge, which is usually between 3 and 5 percent, which is deducted from your initial investment. These funds usually also charge a 12b-1 marketing fee, which is usually around 25 basis points and is deducted from the fund's assets each year. These 12b-1 fees are named for the section of the Investment Company Act that permitted them.
- *B Shares* do not have a front-end load, but carry a redemption fee or back-end load if you redeem shares within a certain number of years. The back-end load declines every year until it disappears (usually after 6 years). B shares carry 12b-1 marketing fees that are typically higher than those on the A shares.
- *C Shares* are known as level-load shares. They do not have front-end or back-end sales charges. They have 12b-1 marketing fees, which are charged as long as you own the fund. There are other classes of funds but they are generally just variations of A, B, and C shares.

Buying mutual funds with loads is one of the biggest rip-offs in the investment industry. Mutual funds with loads have not historically outperformed no-load mutual funds. Paying loads is unnecessarily giving money to a broker. There are plenty of good no-load mutual funds available, running the gamut of investment styles, without even considering a load fund.

See Figure 5.1 for a comparison of a no-load fund and load fund with similar objectives. The no-load fund is the better fund in almost every comparable measure. It has better performance, a portfolio manager with a longer tenure, a lower expense ratio, and it doesn't have a 5.25% load. If one is willing to look, there are no-load funds that are equal or better than any load funds in every investment fund category.

You should also avoid funds with 12b-1 fees. A fund holder should not pay an explicit charge to help a mutual fund company market a fund that the investor already owns. After you bought a Cadillac, would you be willing to pay General Motors a fee so they could advertise the Cadillac brand?

Unlike loads, some expenses of mutual funds cannot be avoided. Money management firms need to generate revenue in some way to stay in business. A fee that every mutual fund firm has that is independent of any sales fee is the *expense ratio*. It is the percentage of a fund's average net assets used to pay its annual administrative and advising expenses. These expenses directly reduce the returns to investors.

The expense ratio incorporates the costs of managing the fund such as salaries and rent, transaction costs, and administrative functions. It is easy to miss because it doesn't appear on your statements as a line-item fee. It is subtracted from your fund's performance behind the scenes. The return given on your statement is after the expense ratio has been deducted from the fund's gross return.

Fixed income funds tend to have lower expense ratios than equity funds and domestic funds tend to have lower expense ratios than international funds. You should target buying no-load stock and bond mutual funds with expense ratios below 1 and international funds with expense ratios below 1.50. For indexed mutual funds, target domestic equity and bond funds with expense ratios below 0.50 and international funds below 1. An expense ratio is a good proxy of the mutual fund's attitude toward its shareholders. If a fund has an outrageously high expense ratio, it probably doesn't have its shareholders best interests in mind. Mutual fund fees and expenses are disclosed, as required by law, in the prospectus of the fund. They are presented in a standardized format, so that you can compare the fees charged by two competing funds. Occasionally, newspapers display what the expense ratios are for the mutual funds that they list in their financial tables.

Figure 5.1 Returns Comparison of a No-Load and a Load Fund with Similar Objectives (As of 12/31/2006)

	No-Load Fund	**Fund with a 5.25% Load**
Fund name	T. Rowe Price Health Sciences Fund	Putnam Health Sciences A Fund
Ticker symbol	PRHSX	PHSTX
Morningstar fund category	Specialty-Health	Specialty-Health
Fund Performance		
1-year returns	9.58%	2.98%
3-year average annual returns	12.95%	7.81%
5-year average annual returns	7.44%	3.40%
10-year average annual returns	12.45%	7.87%
Average annual returns since inception	13.67%	13.08%
Load-adjusted 1-year returns	9.58%	−2.42%
Load-adjusted 3-year Average Annual Returns	12.95%	5.89%
Load-adjusted 5-year average annual returns	7.44%	2.30%
Load-adjusted 10-year average annual returns	12.45%	7.29%
Load-adjusted average annual returns since inception	13.67%	12.83%
Fees and Expenses (As of 12/31/2006)		
No-load/Load	No-load	Load
Expense ratio	0.91%	1.12%
12b-1 fees	0	0.25%
Redemption fee:	N/A	2.00%
Redemption fee on shares held less than	N/A	1 month
Fund Characteristics (As of 12/31/2006)		
Fund advisor	T. Rowe Price Associates	Putnam Investment Management
Fund manager tenure	7 years	2 years
Fund inception date	12/29/1995	05/28/1982
Net assets (millions)	$1,785.46	$1,764.42
Turnover ratio	49.00%	17.00%

Hedge Fund Fees

While mutual funds may or may not be expensive, hedge funds *are* expensive. There is no limit on the fees a hedge fund advisor can charge its limited partners. To manage your money, these so-called masters of the universe typically charge a management fee of between 1% and 2% of your assets under management, plus a performance fee of 20% of a hedge fund's profits. The fee charged by hedge fund managers is often referred to as *2 and 20*. This type of cost structure is a good deal for no one but the hedge funds. See Figure 5.2. They make a ton of money when performance is good, but still get highly compensated when performance is poor. Heads they win; tails you lose.

On top of the high fees, hedge funds have little regulatory oversight and typically limit your ability to redeem your shares. Hedge funds often impose a "lock up" period of a year or more in which you cannot cash in your shares. After that, the funds usually only allow you to redeem them four specific times during the year.

Taxes

Taxes are unfortunately another cost for investors. As the saying goes, "There are two guarantees in life: death and taxes." You may not be able to avoid them but you want to defer them as long as possible.

There is a significant difference between pretax and after-tax returns. Between 1995 and 2005, U.S. equity funds posted an average annual gain of 8.9% before taxes, according to Morningstar. The figure dropped to 7.1% once taxes were paid on distributions. This 1.8% point difference is greater than the expense ratio of most mutual funds.

Figure 5.2 Comparison of Costs for Mutual Funds and Hedge Funds

Mutual Fund		Hedge Fund	
Starting value	$100,000		$100,000
1.00% expense ratio	($1,000)	2% management fee	($2,000)
Value after expense ratio	$99,000	Value after management fee	$98,000
Earns 10% during year	$9,990	Earns 10% during year	$9,800
Value after gains and income for year	$108,990	Value after gains and income for year	$107,800
		Subtract 20% of gains	($1,960)
			$105,840
Fees of $1,000 on initial $100,000 investment		Fees of $3,960 on initial $100,000 investment	

Remember, do not focus on how much you make, but focus on how much you keep. The two taxes that take the biggest chunk out of your investment dollar are capital gains tax and income tax. You pay capital gains tax on assets that have appreciated and have been sold after being held for a year. Your ordinary income tax rate is applied to capital gains for securities held less than a year. In investing, income tax also comes from money earned from coupons and dividends. Income taxes are progressive. The higher your income, the higher your tax bracket, and ultimately the more tax you pay to the government.

Prudent Ways to Cut Your Tax Bill

Everyone likes to keep more of his or her own money and give less to the government. Here are a few ways to legally reduce the amount of taxes you pay on your investments. More money in your pocket is always a good thing. Remember, tax implications should not outweigh your investment analysis in making trading decisions.

Hold Securities More Than 1 Year

Try to hold securities that were recently bought more than 1 year. You will be eligible for long term capital gains that are taxed much more favorably than short term capital gains, which are taxed at your income tax rate. Having a long term approach to the capital markets is helpful in this endeavor. The maximum long term capital gains tax is currently at 15% compared to the maximum income tax rate of 35%. In fact, no matter what your tax basis is, every long term capital gains rate is lower than the corresponding short term rate. See Figure 5.3. The difference between the tax implications of long and short term capital gains rates should be kept in mind if you are considering selling at a gain and you are getting close to qualifying for long term capital gains treatment.

Be aware that a short sale is always considered short term regardless of how long you hold the position. With a short sale the only time the stock is actually held is between when it was bought to cover the position and when you actually delivered the stock to close the position. This length of time is between a few minutes and a few days.

Figure 5.3 Differences between Short and Long Term Capital Gains Rates

Tax Bracket	Short Term Rate	Long Term Rate
10%	10%	5%
15%	15%	5%
25%	25%	15%
28%	28%	15%
33%	33%	15%
35%	35%	15%

Reduce Trading and Buy Funds with Low Turnover

By doing a lower volume of trading, you limit the amount of taxable events. Paper gains are not taxed, only realized gains are. When rebalancing your assets is warranted, try to do it with new money contributions. No taxable events happen when you buy securities.

Besides the amount of taxable events being reduced, by lowing your turnover of securities there is a greater likelihood that the trades that are made will be held for more than a year and subject to the long term capital gains tax rate, instead of the short term rate which is your income tax rate. Constant in and out trading usually only benefits the broker's bottom line, not yours.

You can also reduce the taxes you pay by purchasing index and tax-managed funds which by design consciously try to lower the taxes their fund holders pay. Turnover is much lower in index funds than active funds. The average active mutual fund has an annual turnover rate of 75%. This means that the average holding period for a security in a fund is a year and 4 months. By comparison, the turnover for the S&P 500 has been about 4% historically. Before purchasing a mutual fund ascertain its recent turnover rate.

There are some active mutual funds that make a big effort to keep the taxes that their shareholders will have to pay at a low level. Many times if the fund has a paper loss in some stocks, the portfolio manager might sell those shares to reap the loss, which can then be applied against gains in other stocks the manager has sold. The goal of tax-managed funds is to minimize realized gains, which by law have to be passed on to fund shareholders.

Use Losses Effectively

Unfortunately, sometimes our investments go down in value instead of up. Believe it or not, losses taken in investment securities do provide a benefit. You can take up to $3,000 ($1,500 if married filing separately) of net capital losses each year to reduce your taxable income. If claiming the benefit, there is a 1-month waiting period before you can buy back the security after it was sold. If you have more than $3,000 of net capital loss, it can be carried over to future years. When taking the $3,000 loss, you must take it first from the short term part (if there is one) of your loss.

Buy a Mutual Fund before Its Capital Gains Distribution

You should not buy a mutual fund right before its annual capital gains distribution. The record date is the date set by the issuing company for when you must own shares of a fund to receive a dividend or capital gains distribution. If you buy right before this time, you will be paying tax based on actions that took place before you even owned the fund. The capital gain distribution usually takes place toward the end of the calendar year in November and December. Before investing in a fund, inquire when the capital distribution date is and what the realized gains in the fund are because some mutual fund companies do not disclose this information without some prompting.

Buy Municipal Bonds

Buying municipal bonds instead of corporate and Treasury bonds can cut the amount of taxes you will owe. You should look at the after-tax return of another similarly rated bond before making the decision. If you are in high tax bracket and in a state with a high state income tax, municipal bonds generally provide a higher after-tax return.

Use Some Tax-Advantaged Accounts

Along with having traditional investment accounts, you should have accounts that automatically provide tax benefits. Besides helping achieve a life goal, tax-advantaged accounts such as 401(k) plans, 529 plans, and

IRAs contribute in numerous ways to reduce your tax bill. In some cases they reduce the amount of taxable income you have to report each year. The majority of the capital gains and the income earned in these accounts are not taxed until a much later date. The money invested in these accounts can grow and compound tax-free for a number of years. In the case of the Roth IRA, the contributions made are after-tax but your withdrawals are 100% tax-free.

Give Stocks That Have Appreciated to a Charity

Besides benefiting a cause of your choice, by giving stocks that have appreciated, you avoid paying capital gains tax. You are allowed to write off the full value of the stock when you make the donation.

Be Organized

You should consider keeping your mutual fund and brokerage accounts at only a few firms. The more places you keep your money, the harder and more cumbersome it is to keep track of your accounts. You should try to limit your holdings to four financial institutions. Two banks and two investment firms are all that you need.

Saving all relevant items appropriate for your return is an easy way to possibly cut your tax bill. The cost basis of securities, charitable contributions, and receipts of home office equipment purchases are among a laundry list of items that cannot be used to help lower your tax bill if you have no record of them. You should create a file with all pertinent information and documents for your tax return. If a record or document is not kept, it cannot be used to help lower your taxes.

Points to Remember

- Returns for most investments cannot be predicted. But their costs can be predicted with a fair degree of certainty.
- Discount brokers offer low commissions and provide limited service; full-service brokers charge high commissions and offer extensive handholding.

- Buying stocks through dividend reinvestment plans, or DRIPS, provides a way to bypass brokers. Buying Treasury bonds through Treasury Direct provides another way to bypass brokers.
- Buying mutual funds with loads is one of the biggest rip-offs in the investment industry.
- Some prudent ways to cut your tax bill are:
    - Holding securities more than 1 year
    - Reducing your trading and buying mutual funds with a low turnover rate
    - Utilizing carryover losses
    - Buying a mutual fund before its capital gains distribution
    - Buying municipal bonds, having some accounts that are tax-advantaged
    - Giving stocks that have capital gains to a charity
    - Being organized with your financial documents

CHAPTER 6

THE IMPACT OF ECONOMIC EVENTS ON YOUR PORTFOLIO

Markets can remain irrational longer than you can remain solvent.
JOHN MAYNARD KEYNES

The economy is always changing. Within every 10-year period, there is more than likely going to be a boom period and a recession. Industries are created and some disappear, commodity prices fluctuate, different politicians gain power, and the United States is probably going to be engaged in a war of some kind. The only thing that is certain is that there will be uncertainty.

With so much confusion and so many possible scenarios out there, how should you structure your portfolio? Well, most economic events have occurred before. And although their timing and severity is impossible to predict, you can adjust to certain economic events by observing what has worked well in the past. Of course, there is no guarantee that what worked in the past will work in the future. But history should serve as a starting point.

This chapter is about how you should allocate your assets given various economic scenarios:

- High and low interest rate environments
- Rising and falling interest rate environments
- High and low inflationary environments
- Growing and slowing economic growth
- When a catastrophe happens
- When you receive a windfall

Each scenario is examined in isolation. In the real world, there will be other moving parts that can have an influence on how you manage your money. Also, keep in mind the ever-present investment tagline: "past results are not indicative of future performance."

High Interest Rates

If you are in an environment where there is a high nominal interest rate, anything above 8%, more conservative investments should outperform. You should put more of your money in short term bonds and in money market instruments. Long term bonds and equities generally underperform in a high interest rate environment.

High interest rates increase borrowing costs and makes capital more expensive. It is harder to expand and grow a business when money is more expensive. The sectors in the equity market that hold up the best are defensive sectors such as consumer staples and big pharmaceutical companies. For fixed income securities, there is more default risk when interest rates are high. The higher yield provided by short term cash instruments and short term bonds are competitive to the returns that can be expected from stocks and bonds. It is hard to justify having a large position in equities and in long term bonds when you can get a riskless 8% return in a certificate of deposit.

Low Interest Rates

When interest rates are below 8%, stocks and bonds are usually good assets to own. A study by the CFA Institute found that over the past 39 years, stocks have returned on average about 21.5% a year when the Federal Reserve Bank was keeping rates low and just 2.84% a year when the Fed was tightening rates. The present values of a company's current earnings are higher when interest rates are low. It is easier for corporations to grow when borrowing money is cheap. Some money should be moved out of cash instruments to receive the greater capital appreciation potential that more aggressive assets classes offer in this environment. In general, when rates are low, more risky stocks and bonds are the best performers.

Rising Interest Rates

Short-term bonds and money market instruments should have their weight increased when interest rates are rising. A money market fund is a better choice than a certificate of deposit (CD) because its yield adjusts to the rising rates. A CD cannot take advantage of the rising rates. Whatever the rate was when you bought it is the rate of return you will earn.

When interest rates rise, it's tough sledding for stocks and bonds. The sectors in the equity market that hold up the best are defensive ones such as staples and health care. Many people on Wall Street believe in the "three steps and a stumble" adage. The catch phrase refers to the market's tendency to fall after the Federal Reserve has raised the interest rate three times. A study by the Leuthold Group, the research arm of Weeden & Co., showed that since 1946, stocks have lost on average about 2.7% in the year following the third Fed rate hike. Increasing earnings and growing a business is tougher when rates are rising. Rising rates causes the U.S. dollar to appreciate. Therefore, products that are sold overseas become more expensive to foreign consumers.

The higher interest rates you can earn on cash instruments provide competition for the returns you can expect from the stock market. Bond prices are inversely related to interest rates. See Figure 6.1. This means that when interest rates rise, bond prices decline. Rising rates makes the yield you have on your present bond less attractive compared to a newly issued bond. The poorest performers in a rising interest rate environment are longer term and low-quality bonds.

Falling Interest Rates

When interest rates are declining, stocks and bonds generally perform well. The sectors within both of these asset classes that are especially

Figure 6.1 Bond Prices and Interest Rates (Assuming a 4% Coupon)

Maturity of Bond	After a 1% Increase	After a 1% Decrease	After a 2% Increase	After a 2% Decrease
Short term (2.5 years)	$977	$1,024	$954	$1,049
Intermediate term (10 years)	$922	$1,086	$851	$1,180
Long term (20 years)	$874	$1,150	$769	$1,328

sensitive to interest rates do particularly well. In the equity market, banking and home builder stocks generally outperform. In the fixed income market, long term bonds outperform shorter term bonds when interest rates are falling. Certificates of deposit are a good option for cash in this scenario because the rates you will receive on them here and now will be higher than in the near future when they decline.

High Inflation

When inflation is high, the three main asset classes: stocks, bonds, and cash do not perform well. Of the three assets, stocks do the best. Equities are a decent hedge against rising prices because a company's revenue and earnings should grow at the same level as inflation over time. The purchasing power of your assets is lower when inflation is high. You can buy less for your money. Since they generally offer small nominal returns, a portfolio made up exclusively of cash instruments will struggle to outpace inflation. Principal payments on fixed income investments are worth less when the dollars they are denominated in fall in value.

Real estate and commodities usually buck the trend and perform well in a high inflation environment. They generally move in the same direction as inflation. Gold, in particular, has been viewed as an inflation hedge and a store of value. In the high inflation era of the late 1970s and early 1980s, gold reached its historic high. Businesses that invest in commercial real estate and collect rent are able to benefit from rising rental prices. In addition, if loans are used to purchase properties, rising inflation will benefit the investor, who pays back the debt with cheaper dollars.

The equities that perform the best in this economic scenario are those exposed to commodities and real estate. Real estate investment trusts, oil stocks, and natural resource stocks are examples of equities that perform well. Traditional defensive sectors, such as consumer staples and health care, could also be inflation hedges, especially if the companies can pass along price increases to consumers.

International equities have an edge on domestic equities because foreign goods and services are more competitively priced in this environment. In essence, if consumers want to buy U.S. products they are paying more and getting less. In the global economy we live in, this is not an ideal scenario for U.S. corporations to expand their earnings and profit margins.

Treasury Inflation-Protected Securities (TIPS) are the best choice among fixed income securities when inflation is high. Their principal value is periodically adjusted to the Consumer Price Index, so their exposure to increases in inflation is much less than other bonds. Money market instruments are the best cash option in high inflationary environments. Securities that are liquid and whose interest rates adjust quickly are the best cash instruments during these types of economic times. Money market instruments fit the bill possessing these characteristics.

Low Inflation

In a low inflationary environment, purchasing power is high. Stocks, bonds, and cash perform better under these conditions. It is easier for these asset classes to outpace inflation when inflation is at a low level. More aggressive stocks in sectors such as information technology and consumer discretionary and longer term bonds should be overweighted. Real estate and commodity investments perform relatively poorly during low inflation. When paper money is worth more, real assets usually are worth less.

Growing Economy

When the economy is doing well, more aggressive investments are strong performers. In this scenario, sales and earnings for most companies are growing. Equities, especially in the traditional growth sectors of information technology, consumer discretionary, and biotechnology perform well. Defensive sectors such as consumer staples and utilities should post positive returns in a growing economic environment, but they will likely be underperformers relative to other sectors in the equity space. A growing economy is a good environment for speculative bonds as well. Their default risk is lower when the economy is strong.

The Federal Reserve does its best to try to keep the economy from overheating. The practice that they employ the most is to raise the discount rate to slow the economy down and try to prevent runaway inflation. The major mandate of the Federal Reserve Board is to try to control inflation and to keep the economy growing at a moderate pace.

Recession

When there is an economic slowdown, the best performing stocks are in the more defensive areas of the equity market. You want to be exposed to stocks whose business has little sensitivity to consumers' wallets. People are still going to buy soda and toothpaste if the economy falters. Their cuts will come on discretionary items like dining out or an overseas vacation that may have been planned. Consumer staples, pharmaceutical stocks, and utility stocks should hold up reasonably well during a recession. More aggressive sectors of the stock market will likely be underperformers.

In the fixed income market, lower maturity and safety should be emphasized. Quality bonds with low default risk and short durations are good choices. Treasury bills and notes have the characteristics that satisfy these criteria.

Real estate generally will not be a strong performer in a recession because of lower demand. Rents and mortgage payments become more burdensome to pay. The result is that foreclosures spike during economic slowdowns.

Catastrophe Strikes

A natural disaster, a terrorist attack, a major financial fraud: no one knows when and where a catastrophe is going to happen. Unfortunately, we can be very confident that they will occur in the future and that they will have a major impact on the financial markets and on your investments. The key to preparing your finances for this type of event is to be proactive and do it before the disaster occurs. The best way to do this is to already have a diverse portfolio.

No single stock or bond should make up more than 10% of your portfolio. Furthermore, no asset class should represent more than 75% of your net worth. For example, even if there is a stock market crash as in 1987 where the market declines 20% in one day, if your assets consist of more than just equities you will take a financial hit but not get financially wiped out. Some of your other assets outside the stock market will hold up better. It is virtually impossible for Treasury bonds and money market instruments to have a 20% decline in a single day. Having your assets spread around beforehand will reduce the chance that you act hastily and do something financially stupid. You have to try to think beyond the devastating moment at hand. Panicking never made anyone rich. In most cases, the financial markets have eventually rebounded after a catastrophe.

Receiving a Windfall

Some of us will have our finances get a boost unexpectedly at some point in our lives. It may be the result of a big bonus at work or an inheritance from a loved one. The number of times in your life that you receive this type of financial good fortune will probably be low. Do not squander this opportunity to improve your financial health.

My suggestion is not to act hastily when the money comes into your possession. Avoid the urge to splurge. Do not immediately go out and purchase an expensive discretionary item.

I recommend putting the money in a safe money market fund for a few months while you contemplate how to use the windfall. This will allow you to earn a little interest and delay making an important decision to a time when you may be a little less emotional and more rational about a proper use of the money.

My suggestion is to incorporate the windfall into your overall financial goals. Try to look at the money as a paycheck, not a gift. Prioritize what would give the biggest boost to your financial health. Paying off high interest loans, especially credit card debt should be high on your list of financial moves to make. If debt is not a concern, boosting your retirement and college savings and adding to your emergency fund are smart moves. Three to six months of your expenses should be the amount targeted for your emergency fund. If these accounts are in sound order, consider using the new money to rebalance your portfolio. Increase the weights of some of your underperforming asset classes to your initial allocation. By adding new money you avoid taxes that would occur if you rebalanced by selling securities.

Points to Remember

- Conservative investments such as short term Treasury bonds and money market accounts should outperform in a high, or rising, or both high and rising interest rate environment.
- Stocks and long term bonds usually perform well when interest rates are lower, falling, or both.
- Money market funds are better than a CD when interest rates are rising because their yield adjusts to the rising rates.
- Equities are a decent hedge against inflation; real estate and commodities usually are the star performers in an inflationary environment.
- When the economy is doing well, more aggressive investments are strong performers. In an economic slowdown, the more defensive instruments do the best.
- The best way to prepare your finances for a catastrophic event is to be proactive by being diversified ahead of time.
- If you receive a windfall, put it in a money market fund for a few months while you decide how to invest it. Think through how these new assets can best improve your financial situation.

PART II

DETERMINING YOUR ASSET ALLOCATION MIX

CHAPTER 7

THE THREE PRIMARY FACTORS IN DETERMINING YOUR ALLOCATION MIX

YOUR STAGE OF LIFE, WHEN YOU WILL NEED THE MONEY, AND YOUR RISK TOLERANCE

The biggest risk in investing is doing nothing at all.

CHARLES SCHWAB

The great hockey player Wayne Gretzky once said the key to being a successful hockey player was not knowing where the puck is but where it will be. The same logic applies to managing your money. In the investment world, asset allocation is the process that takes your assets from where they are now to where they should be in the future.

There are three main issues that you should consider when dividing up your assets: your stage of life, when you will need the money, and your risk tolerance. Obviously, other circumstances will influence your asset allocation decision, but these three primary factors are a solid starting point to figure out what type of assets and what percentage of these assets you should have in your portfolio.

First Factor: Your Stage of Life

Asset allocation is not a static process. You cannot just divide up your portfolio and leave it on autopilot for the rest of your life. You should have an initial plan and expect to make adjustments along the way. Life events will occur which may prompt you to change your asset mix. Death, sickness, job loss, and divorce happen, as well as happy moments such as births, marriage, promotions, and graduations. In a nutshell, as life goes along, many things are going to happen.

A good place to start is to look at your job and your family situation. Beginning with more quantifiable factors allows you to form a foundation for setting up your portfolio, before having to consider the murkier ones. You know what stage of life you are in. *What is important is your stage of life, not your age.* Your age and stage of life do not always correspond. You should also take into consideration the number of dependents you have and what their financial needs are.

A smart way to divide your life into stages is to focus on where you are in your career path. This is a universal approach, since most adults have to work, while not all get married or have children. Your working years are the primary period when you accumulate assets. What you do with your assets during this period will go a long way in determining what your lifestyle will be like now and in the future. I have divided the life stages into four distinct periods: early career, middle career, late career approaching retirement, and retirement. The majority of people will be in all of these stages during their lifetimes and will pass through them sequentially. The exact timing of these life stages will vary for different people. Again, these stages are your early career, your middle career, your late career, and your retirement.

Early Career

Prime objective: Setting up and funding your investment accounts
Major fear: Debt getting out of control

You should start to think about investments and asset allocation when you receive your first paycheck. You should not even wait for your first "real" job after you have completed your education. The first time you get paid for doing a newspaper route, babysitting, or any seasonal or summer job you should consider what you are going to do with your earnings. Most teenagers will focus on buying discretionary items such as an iPod or the latest hip pair of blue jeans. You should save and invest part of your earnings, even if it is only a small amount of money.

Part-time work in your youth offers many benefits. It teaches responsibility, gives you exposure to the real world, and also teaches you how difficult it is to make a living. Many of the most successful people in the world had jobs in their youth.

Kids are usually horrified to see how much taxes are taken out of a paycheck. Part-time work can demonstrate firsthand what kind of work you may and may not want to do for the rest of your life. In many cases you will reach the conclusion that the way to get the skills you need to go where you want to go is through education.

Low earnings and high expenses usually characterize the early career stage, when you begin working full-time. The majority of people are single at this point and have some debt. It is very important at this early stage to think about saving and investing because good habits start young and can form a foundation for a lifetime. Furthermore, by starting young the power of compounding really works in your favor. In terms of your finances, by investing at a young age you can get a big leg up on your peers. Delayed short-term gratification usually results in increased satisfaction over the long term.

Figure 7.1 demonstrates the power of compounding combined with starting early. In the example, the early saver contributes $5,000 a year between the ages of 20 and 30 and then nothing more, and the other person contributes $5,000 a year between the ages of 30 and 60. Assuming a constant 8% return, the early contributor ends up with significantly more money at age 60 than the later contributor. This result occurs despite the fact that the later contributor put in $150,000 in the account and the early contributor put in only $50,000. The lesson to take from the example is: the earlier you start your retirement savings, the less you usually will have to put aside in the long run.

When you finish your formal education and get your first "real" job, there are a number of moves you should make to put yourself on firm financial ground. You should establish a written budget. You need to quantify what your assets are and what income you are bringing in. You also need to see what your monthly expenses are and in what areas it can be prudent to try to reduce them.

Figure 7.1 The Power of Compounding (Assuming a Constant 8% Return)

| Age | Early Saver | | Late Saver | |
---	Contribution	Value	Contribution	Value
20	$5,000	$5,400		
21	$5,000	$11,232		
22	$5,000	$17,531		
23	$5,000	$24,333		
24	$5,000	$31,680		
25	$5,000	$39,614		
26	$5,000	$48,183		
27	$5,000	$57,438		
28	$5,000	$67,433		
29	$5,000	$78,227		
30	$5,000	$84,486	$5,000	$5,400
31		$91,244	$5,000	$11,232
32		$98,544	$5,000	$17,531
33		$106,428	$5,000	$24,333
34		$114,942	$5,000	$31,680
35		$124,137	$5,000	$39,614
36		$134,068	$5,000	$48,183
37		$144,794	$5,000	$57,438
38		$156,377	$5,000	$67,433
39		$168,887	$5,000	$78,227
40		$182,398	$5,000	$89,886
41		$196,990	$5,000	$102,476
42		$212,749	$5,000	$116,075
43		$229,769	$5,000	$130,761
44		$248,151	$5,000	$146,621
45		$268,003	$5,000	$163,751
46		$289,443	$5,000	$182,251
47		$312,598	$5,000	$202,231
48		$337,606	$5,000	$223,810
49		$364,615	$5,000	$247,115
50		$393,784	$5,000	$272,284
51		$425,287	$5,000	$299,466
52		$459,310	$5,000	$328,824
53		$496,054	$5,000	$360,530
54		$535,739	$5,000	$394,772
55		$578,598	$5,000	$431,754
56		$624,886	$5,000	$471,694
57		$674,876	$5,000	$514,830
58		$728,867	$5,000	$561,416
59		$787,176	$5,000	$611,729
60		$850,150	$5,000	$666,068

What can you reasonably afford in your housing expense: namely, your rent or mortgage payment. Housing is generally the biggest expense for people at this stage. The goal is to transition from a renter to a homeowner.

At this stage you also need to determine what type of debt you have and what the interest rates on your loans are. Many at this stage have student and car loans. Do your best to pay down any debts you have in a timely manner.

An emergency fund covering 3 months of expenses should be established in an attempt to mitigate financial hardship, in the case some unforeseen event occurs. Expect the unexpected. The emergency fund should be kept in a safe and liquid money market fund that earns a little interest. If you need to tap into the emergency fund you should try to replenish it as soon as you can.

Insurance is needed to protect your valuable assets, including your earning power. Specifically, health insurance is a must for everyone no matter your stage in life. Car and property insurance is essential for anyone who owns or rents a home and drives a car. Lastly, life insurance is only needed for those who have dependents, no one else.

Even though it may seem like retirement is a long way off, if you are just starting out you should set up a retirement account and contribute as much as you can afford. Less than half of eligible workers participate in 401(k) plans in their twenties, according to Hewitt Associates. As demonstrated in Figure 7.1, by starting early compounding can really work its magic. If your employer offers a retirement plan strongly consider contributing to it, especially if it offers a company match. The money being automatically taken out of your paycheck provides forced savings and a convenient way to dollar cost average. Money not seen cannot be spent and in a lot of cases wasted. Automated investment programs make it easy to continue investing regardless of any potential variations in your financial picture.

A Roth IRA is another good option. Of the retirement vehicles available, it provides the most flexibility for withdrawing your money with the fewest penalties. Most individuals who are just starting off in the working world will satisfy the Roth's somewhat stringent income requirement to contribute. Single filers can contribute and get the full benefits of a Roth as long as their adjusted gross income is less than $110,000. As your career advances and hopefully you are making more money, a Roth IRA may not be available as an option. You will be thanking yourself in your retirement years for setting up this type of account because you will able to withdraw from it totally tax-free.

It is important for 20-something investors to segregate their traditional and retirement accounts. These two types of accounts should be invested very differently. Your retirement account should be invested aggressively with a large percentage in equities. Small-cap, mid-cap, and international stocks should represent up to 75% of the overall equity component. Time is your greatest ally, with retirement approximately 40 years away. At this stage, the great enemy of your retirement account is inflation. Over the long term, stocks have proven to be the best inflation beater.

Your traditional taxable account should be invested much more conservatively. Paying off student loan debt and saving for a down payment on a home are two common objectives for many at this stage. Money market funds, cash instruments, and quality bonds should make up at least 40% of the holdings in traditional accounts. These types of assets will help you have some liquidity, which is usually needed in your traditional accounts at this stage.

Just as compounding and time can work wonders for your investable assets, it can cause financial havoc if you have a lot of debt. You need to make sure you do not bite off more than you can chew with home, car, and student loans. Debt should be mainly used to acquire assets that have the potential to appreciate, such as real estate, educational services, or a business.

You have to be especially careful about not abusing your credit cards. Debt on credit cards has an average annualized interest rate of about 18%. You will be hard pressed to find any investment that will consistently have that high a return. Card issuers market to young people incessantly. Visit any college campus and you will see this firsthand. Statistics show younger people are more likely to be late with their credit card payments or to just pay the minimum on their balance. This piles up interest and profits for the card issuer but is very expensive for the cardholder.

If you use your credit card wisely, you can save thousands of dollars over your lifetime. Paying off debt on time leads to higher credit scores. Having a high credit score is particularly important because you may want to take out loans for high-priced, first-time purchases such as a home or car. A higher credit score will allow you to get a lower interest rate to borrow for these items, saving you large sums of money.

You can get a free credit report from the three major credit reporting agencies. Equifax, Experian, and TransUnion have created a website AnnualCreditReport.com which allows you one free credit report per year from each reporting agency. With the increasing threat of identity theft and just for your own knowledge, you should take advantage of this service.

A rewards card is a good choice for your primary credit card if you are very attentive in paying off your bill on time. Benefits such as cash back, airlines miles, or contributions into a college savings account are among the gamut of rewards that are available. When choosing a card select one that offers a reward that provides some value to you and whose interest rate is reasonable, just in case you are late on a payment. Avoid cards that charge an annual fee.

Lastly, one of the good habits to start when you are in your early career is to review your portfolio periodically. You should do a review at least once a year, preferably quarterly. By looking at your portfolio a few times over the course of the year you will notice quickly if your desired asset allocation is still intact. If it is not, you may choose to rebalance your assets. Whenever an asset class drifts 5% away from its desired allocation, a rebalancing should be considered.

Middle Career Years

Prime objective: Segregating money to invest and getting good performance from it
Major fear: Career not progressing as you had hoped

There is no set age when your middle career years happen. It usually occurs in your 30s and 40s. This stage generally sees an increase in your earning power, coinciding with high expenses. Besides having your plate filled at work, there are a lot of financial responsibilities to be taken care of at home. Most people are married and are raising children during this period. It costs a middle-income family approximately $250,000 to raise a child from birth to age 17, according to a recent study by the U.S. Department of Agriculture. This high cost doesn't include the cost of college. Furthermore, some people in this middle career stage sometimes have the dual responsibility of caring for their kids and their elderly parents. This group sometimes is referred to as the "sandwich generation."

You need to make sure your overall insurance coverage is adequate at this stage. You want your heirs to be financially protected in case you prematurely pass away. Do not buy a life insurance policy with an investment component. The fees on these products, which include universal life, variable life, and whole life, are exorbitant.

Your life insurance choice should be *term insurance*, which gives you the most coverage for the lowest price. Remember, the purpose of life insurance is to replace the income of the deceased when someone is dependent on that income.

You should continue funding your retirement account, and if you have children, you should establish an educational account such as a 529 plan. It is imperative if you change jobs that you do not cash out of your retirement plan. Cashing out of a retirement plan will trigger large tax liabilities. You should roll your plan into an IRA or into your new employer's plan. Furthermore, a will should be established to designate how you want your assets dispersed. An executor should be named and a guardian appointed for your minor children.

Both retirement and education accounts should be invested aggressively with a high component in equities because of the return potential and the money not being needed for a number of years. That being said, some risk control and capital preservation should take place in these tax-advantaged accounts. Compared to the early career stage, there should be a slight increase in high-quality bonds and safe cash instruments. Your emergency fund should be increased to cover 6 months of expenses because of the likelihood of more dependents and responsibilities in the middle career stage.

As your tax-advantaged accounts get slightly more conservative in the middle career stage, your taxable accounts should become slightly more aggressive. Generally, there is a bigger pool of discretionary money to work with at this point in your life. For individuals in high tax brackets, municipal bonds become a viable option for part of your regular taxable portfolio. Your equity position can be raised slightly because generally liquidity is not as much of a concern as it was earlier. Index funds and stocks you plan to hold for a while are a good choice for the equity portion of a taxable account. All things being equal, having investments with low expenses and that generate a low amount of taxes will raise your total return substantially. Costs can be predicted much more accurately than capital gains going forward.

Late Career: Approaching Retirement

Prime objective: Making the most out of your highest earning years
Major fear: Not having enough money to retire on

Your career will probably taper off when you are between the ages of 50 and 65. These are also the years when you will probably be earning the highest salary of your career. Your expenses during these late career years will likely by lower. That's because your mortgage tends to be close to fruition and your children are usually on their own or close to being independent. If you have been lax funding your retirement accounts, this is the time to step up and increase your contributions because time is running out. If you are age 50 or older, the government grants you a catch-up provision that allows you to contribute more to a 401(k) and IRA than is normally allowed.

Your insurance needs will change slightly at this stage. As children get older, you do not need as much life insurance. Like in all stages, health and property insurance are still must haves.

You should buy long term disability insurance at this stage. Income, especially since it is likely to be high, needs to be protected in case of a disability. Unfortunately, the chance of a long term disability increases at this stage in your life. These policies pay up to 60% of your salary if you are unable to work.

Both your taxable and tax-advantaged portfolios should become slightly more conservative during this stage. Moving 5% to 10% out of equities into fixed income and money market accounts is wise; it will still give you significant exposure to stocks but help reduce some of your market risk and volatility. The return potential of equities and their historical ability to outpace inflation makes holding stocks a must in your portfolio. Realize that if you are in your 40s or 50s, you likely have a time horizon of 30 to 40 years.

With the higher income that many are earning at this stage, municipal bonds should be considered for a portion of the fixed-income allocation in your traditional account because of the tax benefits they provide. Your income tax rate is generally at its highest during this stage.

If you are close to the end of your career, you should do an inventory on what assets and liabilities you have. Retirement is approaching and it is imperative for you to see what you currently have that you can live on when you stop working. In terms of your assets, you need to have a good estimate of what you can expect from a pension, your retirement accounts, your regular accounts, and Social Security benefits. You can order a statement from the Social Security Administration that estimates your benefits by calling 1-800-772-1213 or going to www.ssa.gov on the Internet.

You should start to think about where you want to live and what you are going to be doing with your time in retirement. You need to ask yourselves questions like these: Do you want to live in the same house or move to a more affordable house? Do you want to continue working full-time, part-time, or not at all? Do you want to travel extensively? At what age do you plan to collect Social Security benefits? What tax bracket do you think you will be in during retirement? To meet your retirement goals at this stage, you may need to save more, to take more risk in your portfolio, or to work longer than you intended to.

Retirement

Prime objective: Maintain lifestyle at same level as before retirement
Major fear: Running out of money

In the 1970s movie *The Candidate* with Robert Redford, Redford's character goes through the trials and tribulations of a long, tough senatorial campaign. After winning a close election, Redford turns to an aide and utters the famous line "Now what?" When you finally reach retirement, you do not want to say those words. You should do a lot of planning and consider many things before retiring.

At this stage, you shift gears from asset accumulation to asset withdrawal and preservation. The major financial concern of retirees is longevity risk—having your assets dwindle while you still need income. During retirement, you typically receive income from three sources: Social Security, employer-sponsored retirement accounts, such as a 401(k) or a pension plan, and personal accounts and investments including IRAs. Currently, you can start to collect Social Security at age 62. If you wait until age 67, you will get the maximum benefits. See Figure 7.2. In the future, these ages will most likely be raised.

If you are getting Social Security benefits when you turn 65, your Medicare hospital benefits start automatically. If you are not getting Social Security benefits, you should sign up for Medicare close to your

Figure 7.2 Social Security Retirement Benefits

		Annual Retirement Benefits		
Year Attained Age 65	Full Retirement Age	At Full Retirement Age*	Age 62*	Age 70
2006	65†	$24,685	$18,437	$34,184
2010	66	$25,732	$18,794	$35,250
2015	66	$28,325	$20,762	$38,284
2025	67	$31,887	$22,007	$40,178
2035	67	$35,498	$24,536	$44,708
2045	67	$39,552	$27,347	$49,809

*Assumes January 2 date of birth.
†Full retirement age in 2006 would actually be 65 plus 8 months.
Source: Social Security Administration, 2006 Trustees Report Assumptions.

65th birthday, even if you will not be retired by that time. For those with traditional IRAs, distributions must be made by the calendar year after you turn 70½ or you face stiff IRS penalties.

You need to make sure—before you stop working—that you will be able to generate enough income to maintain a decent lifestyle in retirement. You need to have a good idea how you are going to spend your time. When you retire by choice, it is difficult to return to the workforce later on at a salary as high as the salary you were receiving before retiring. Unfortunately in many cases people do not leave work on their own terms. According to an Employee Benefit Research Institute 2004 Retirement Confidence Survey, 37% of retirees leave work before they had planned to, often because of health, layoffs, or other problems outside of their control.

When you stop working, you do not have the support of your full-time paycheck and need to make do on your other sources of funds. You should look to draw down your retirement accounts at the rate of no more than 4% per year, especially in the first few years of retirement. You should increase this to include the effects of inflation in subsequent years. A major goal of retirees is for the annual return on your investments to be greater than the percentage that you withdraw. If this is accomplished, a steady stream of income will be generated and your principal can continue to grow.

Withdrawals should take place from your nontaxable accounts before taking money from your taxable accounts. This way, your money in 401(k) plans and traditional IRAs continues to grow, tax-deferred. It is important to watch your expenses, and live within your means. Time is not on your side anymore. At this stage, mistakes made managing your money are not easily repaired. To supplement their income and take up some of their time, many seniors decide to work part-time. When you reach this stage, you want working to be your choice, not something you must do to pay your bills.

Even though people receive Medicare, health care costs during this period are high. According to the March 2006 Fidelity Retiree Health Care Cost Estimate, a couple retiring at age 65 without an employer-funded retirement health plan in place, will need $200,000 to supplement Medicare and out-of-pocket-health care costs over the course of their retirement. Luckily, most other expenses are lower at this point.

For most at the retirement stage, preservation of capital is the primary financial goal. Investments which generate income with little risk of the loss of principal are a popular choice. High-quality bonds should make up a large portion of your portfolio. High-yielding stocks, REITs, and lower-quality bonds should also be part of the mix.

Because you can expect to be living longer and spending more time in retirement, you can't ignore the growth rate of your capital. You should first make sure you can have and maintain a decent quality of life over a number of years while getting Social Security and your other sources of retirement income. Once you are satisfactorily getting by, you can start thinking of growing part of your portfolio. If you have accumulated more money than you will ever need in retirement, stocks can be a significant portion of your portfolio. The time frame of a person who is primarily concerned with how to pass the assets down to the next generation or to a charity is much longer than the average retiree.

The four stages of the process discussed in this chapter is just a starting point in deciding your asset allocation mix. It is by no means a one-size-fits-all process. The demographics of our society are changing. People are living longer, marrying and starting families later in life, having fewer children, and switching jobs more often. You will likely experience all of the four stages during your life and you will face many of the issues presented. Knowing what stage you are in can give you an idea of what financial issues you will be facing now and in the future. This will ultimately help you organize your investment portfolio. After having established where you are in your life and career, the two primary factors in determining your asset allocation are when you are going to need the money and your risk tolerance.

Second Factor: When the Money Will Be Needed

It bears repeating that you should segregate your accounts. Different investment accounts should have different objectives. For example, you should have your retirement account completely separate from your regular taxable discretionary investment account. This is important because the timing of when the money will be needed and the risk you can take for your separate accounts, and hence the asset allocation applied to them, can be very different from one account to another. Commingling all your investments is a big mistake. For example, if you are just starting out you should have your retirement account invested very differently than an account used to save up for a down payment on your first house.

Your investing time horizon is the expected number of months, years, or decades you will be investing to achieve a particular goal. The time at which the money will be needed and spent helps determine the flexibility you have in accumulating and managing it. In isolation, money that will be needed within 3 years should be invested very differently from money that will be needed in 15 years. Some chances can be taken and money can be managed aggressively if it will not be needed for a number of years. There is time to make up any investment mistakes that are made. The longer you can hold an investment, the more chance there is that the long-term growth in returns will overcome the short-term ups and downs in performance. The ability to hold an investment long term helps you tolerate more volatile investments and take advantage of the higher return potential they provide.

If the money is going to be used for something important in the short term, it should be invested very conservatively. There should be no chance of loss of principal. A sharp drop in the value of an investment just before the money is needed can cause a shortfall that cannot be made up. You should never have to start a conversation: "Dear, we cannot retire next year because I lost half our money in the stock market over the past month."

Long term goals over time turn into short term goals. You should make sure that you adjust your portfolio accordingly. In most cases, investments that are initially aggressive should become more conservative as they approach the target date when the money will be needed. This usually entails shifting funds from equities to more conservative fixed income and cash instruments.

Third Factor: Your Risk Tolerance

The last of the primary determinants that should go into your asset allocation decision is your risk tolerance. Of the three primary factors, your risk tolerance is the most subjective. Some individuals have strong feelings about how much risk they can tolerate. Others need some guidance to find out the amount of risk they are willing to take on. Figures 7.3 and 7.4 are two sample risk questionnaires that can help you ascertain your investment risk comfort. For them to provide any value to you, it is important for you to answer the questions honestly.

The two main investment risks for you are *market risk* and *inflation risk*. Another way of saying this is that the two risks you should worry about are that the overall stock or bond market goes down and that your investments do not keep up with inflation. The two aspects of life that you have to deal with here are the uncertainty of future events and the difficulty of maintaining your purchasing power. Most people see risk simply as the chance that their investments will lose money. Many view a decline in their portfolio of 5% as very bad, even if the relevant benchmark was down 20%.

Common risk measures in the investment world are standard deviation, tracking error, and value at risk. *Standard deviation* tells the investor the extent the investor's returns deviate from the mean. The greater the deviation from the mean, the higher the portfolio risk. Standard deviation is commonly used as the risk component in measuring risk-adjusted performance of a portfolio such as in the Sharpe Ratio. The formula for the Sharpe Ratio is the return on the portfolio minus the risk-free rate divided by the standard deviation of the portfolio. The measurement is useful because although one portfolio can reap higher returns than its peers, it is only a good investment if those returns do not come with too much additional risk. The higher the Sharpe Ratio is for a portfolio, the greater its risk-adjusted performance has been. A variation of the Sharpe Ratio is the Sortino Ratio, which removes the effects of upward price movements on standard deviation to instead measure only return against downward price volatility. You should be more concerned with the volatility that come from negative returns than those that come from large positive returns.

Tracking error is calculated as the standard deviation of the differences between the portfolio returns and the benchmark returns, thereby

Figure 7.3 Questionnaire to Determine Risk Tolerance

Instructions: Circle your answer to each of these questions:

1. What kind of gain are you expecting from your investments?
    A. 4%
    B. 7%
    C. 10%
    D. 15%
    E. 20%

2. Which scenario would you choose if you had the choice?
    A. 100% chance of $25,000
    B. 50% chance of $35,000 and 50% chance of $15,000
    C. 50% chance of $50,000 and 50% chance of $0
    D. 25% chance of $100,000 and 75% chance of $0
    E. 5% chance of $500,000 and 95% chance of $0

3. If you bought an investment a month a go and it rose 100% since, what would you do?
    A. Sell the whole position
    B. Sell part of position
    C. Set a price point where if it falls to you would sell
    D. Do nothing
    E. Buy more

4. If you bought an investment a month a go and it went down 50%, what would you do?
    A. Sell the whole position
    B. Sell part of position
    C. Set a price point where if it falls to you would sell
    D. Do nothing and go down with the ship
    E. Buy more

5. What is your main goal when you invest your money?
    A. Preserve capital; no loss of value would be acceptable
    B. Create current income in safe investments
    C. Have growth in investments as well as income

    D. Willing to take some risks if there is chance of strong relative performance

    E. Willing to take large risks if there is chance of huge gains

6. I prefer an investment with little or no ups and downs in value, and I am willing to accept the lower returns these investments provide.

    A. Strongly Agree

    B. Agree

    C. Somewhat Agree

    D. Disagree

    E. Strongly Disagree

7. If you could choose only one investment vehicle in the stock market, what would it be?

    A. Wouldn't invest in stock market; it is too risky

    B. Mutual funds

    C. Individual stocks

    D. Hedge funds

    E. Call and put options

Grading Instructions: Convert: A = 1, B = 2, C = 3, D = 4, E = 5. Take the sum of answers and divide by 7. Round to the nearest whole number.

Grading:

1 = very low risk tolerance

2 = low risk tolerance

3 = moderate risk tolerance

4 = high risk tolerance

5 = extremely high risk tolerance.

Figure 7.4 Questionnaire to Determine Risk Profile

Instructions: For each of the following questions circle one answer:

1 = Strongly Agree 2 = Agree 3 = Somewhat Agree 4 = Disagree 5 = Strongly Disagree

1. I do not get angry if an investment of mine loses value.
   1 2 3 4 5

2. Putting money into mutual funds or stocks and following the result is a form of recreation as well as an investment.
   1 2 3 4 5

3. I'm willing to risk losing part of my investment if there is also the chance of a big reward.
   1 2 3 4 5

4. I'm never short of cash at the end of a pay period.
   1 2 3 4 5

5. I'd rather have a 20% chance of making $10,000 than a 100% chance of making $2,000.
   1 2 3 4 5

6. No matter what happens to my investments, I know I'll always have enough money to live comfortably.
   1 2 3 4 5

7. If I won $30,000, I'd invest it in the stock market.
   1 2 3 4 5

8. Savings accounts are a waste of time. If you're going to stay ahead of inflation, you need to make aggressive investments.
   1 2 3 4 5

9. I do not mind charging my credit cards right to the limit because I feel I'll always be able to find the money to pay them off.
   1 2 3 4 5

10. If my employer gave me a choice between a pension plan
    that guaranteed a moderate retirement income or a plan that
    might either make me very rich at retirement or leave me
    very little, I'd take a chance on the second plan.
    1 2 3 4 5

Grading Instructions: Take the average of your answers and
round to the nearest whole number to see what your risk profile is.

Grading:
1 = extremely aggressive
2 = moderately aggressive
3 = moderate
4 = moderately conservative
5 = extremely conservative

measuring how widely the portfolio returns deviate from the benchmark. There is a problem if the tracking error is not low for an S&P
500 Index Fund whose benchmark is the S&P 500.

Value at risk (VaR) quantifies the potential loss which, at a predetermined probability and over a set time frame, should not be exceeded
provided that the composition of the portfolio remains the same. A daily
VaR of –5% at 99% confidence means that on only 1 of every 100 days
will a loss be expected to exceed the –5% mark.

With all these risk measures, the thing to watch out for is outliers.
Extreme events will happen in the future that will affect your portfolios return. Relationships that have worked in the past may not hold in
the future. Furthermore, new factors and asset classes may emerge that
could bring new dimensions into the market.

It is imperative that you feel comfortable with your investments. If
you are risk averse and would be very upset with a capital loss, you
should limit the amount of equities in your portfolio. Your psychological makeup needs to be strongly considered. Some people are comfortable taking risks; others are not. There is also a wide spectrum of
attitudes about risk in between.

You need to clearly understand the possible outcomes of an investment strategy. If you cannot handle some of the possible scenarios, you should reconsider your investment strategy. Your recent investment experience should not cloud your judgment. For example, recent success may bias you toward taking on more risk than is appropriate, while recent setbacks may push you to take a more conservative approach. Overall, your attitude toward risk *must* be a major factor in deciding on how your assets are divided. I think it is best for an investor to try to be level-headed. Do not get overly confident in your ability after good results or too pessimistic after a series of bad returns.

The three primary factors discussed can be applied to everyone. In helping to allocate your money, many other factors can also have an influence on this decision. Some of these secondary factors such as your income and your health status are somewhat incorporated in the primary factors. As you get older, you usually become wealthier and less healthy. It is always important to remember that everyone is unique. You have different aspirations, worries, and influences. Ultimately, everyone has a different set of people that they love and want to help take care of financially.

Points to Remember

- Your stage of life, when you will need your money, and your risk tolerance are the three primary factors in deciding how you should divide up your assets.
- You should have an initial asset allocation plan and expect to make adjustments to that plan along the way.
- In your early career, your prime objective should be setting up and funding your investment accounts. Your major fear is your debts getting out of control.
- In your middle career years, your prime objective should be segregating money to invest for retirement and getting good performance from it. Your major fear is that your career is not progressing as you had hoped.
- When you are in the late stages of your career, your prime objective should be making the most out of your high earning years. Your major fear is not having enough money to retire on.

- In retirement your prime objective is maintaining your lifestyle at the same level as before retirement and your major fear is running out of money.
- If you figure out when you will spend your money, it will give you more flexibility in accumulating and managing it.
- Of the three primary factors used to determine your asset allocation mix, your risk tolerance is the most subjective.

CHAPTER 8

THE SIX SECONDARY FACTORS THAT INFLUENCE HOW YOU CONSTRUCT YOUR PORTFOLIO

YOUR AGE, GENDER, MARITAL STATUS, INVESTING EXPERIENCE, DEPENDENTS, AND AFFLUENCE

The essence of investment management is the management of risks, not the management of returns.

BENJAMIN GRAHAM

What stage are you in your career? What is your time horizon? What is your comfort level with risk? The answers to these three key questions determine how you allocate your assets and serve as a framework for how your money should be divided. There are, however, many other circumstances that can influence how you tilt your portfolio.

In this chapter I discuss some of the circumstances, or secondary factors, that should be considered in determining your asset allocation. Each of the factors is discussed in isolation, but be aware that there are also some shades of gray between some of the comparisons presented.

You should know where your money is and how it is being invested. Furthermore, you should determine who could best handle your assets if you are unable to do so. No matter who you are, keep these universal money management rules in mind:

- Clearly define what your investment objective is.
- Strive to get the highest return with the lowest amount of risk.
- Keep costs under control.
- Diversify the asset classes you invest in and diversify within the asset classes.
- Know yourself.
- Track the performance of your investments.
- Be patient.

Young versus Old

All things being equal, the younger you are, the more aggressive you can be with your money. The time to take some chances is when you are in your 20s and 30s. This is especially true with accounts that have long term goals. Aggressive does not mean stupid and careless. Your decisions should be well thought out.

Time is on your side when you are younger. The majority of your working years are in front of you. If you have poor returns in some years, there is more than enough time for your portfolio to catch up. You can be reasonably confident that the good years will more than offset the bad years over the long term.

During your early career, your income is usually relatively low. Debt should be kept in check and only used for essential items. It is imperative that you budget and set aside money for investing. The advantage of having a long time frame cannot be utilized if you are not putting money in the financial markets. Compounding of your money cannot occur if there is no money to compound.

Equities, including small cap and international issues, should make up the bulk of a young person's accounts with long term goals. If a young person feels comfortable with real estate and commodities, they can also have a place in the investor's long term portfolio. Home ownership should be one of the major financial goals of the young.

It needs to be emphasized, no matter what a person's age, that assets which are designated for imminent important goals should be in very safe instruments. No chances should be taken. Young people often have short term goals such as saving for the down payment on a house and paying off student loans. This usually means placing money in safe and liquid fixed income and money market instruments that can be used for these upcoming purposes. Whether you are 21 or 81, no money that is needed in 3 months for something important should be exposed to the stock market.

As you get older, you should have a more conservative outlook for your assets. The great fear of people as they get older is that they will run out of their money. Even with the assistance of the government programs, it is safe to assume that as a person ages their health care costs will increase. Also, your health as you enter your senior years is more unpredictable. It is difficult to know exactly when you will need a large sum for health care expenses. This uncertainty should lead one to be more cautious than a healthy younger person.

Most older people have accumulated some assets, but their working years are dwindling. Asset preservation and income generation become more important the older a person gets. The main goal is to have your nest egg and other sources of retirement income provide enough for you during your golden years. A portion of your money should be shifted to fixed income and money market instruments. Equities should still encompass a significant part of an older person's portfolio because of the growth and inflation protection they provide.

People are living longer and spending more time in retirement so the growth of the assets in their portfolio should not be ignored. Growth and income investments are particularly attractive for the elderly. There are individual equities and funds that can provide both capital appreciation potential and a decent yield.

It is also imperative for adults, especially the elderly, to have a will to map out how they want their assets distributed when they pass away. Such an instrument gives you the peace of mind that comes from knowing that you will ultimately determine where your money is going, not a court. A good addition to a will is a living revocable trust. It provides a great way to manage your assets when you are alive and makes the inheritance process smoother for your heirs.

Male versus Female

Whether you are a man or a woman influences how you set up your portfolio. The different personality and emotional traits of men and women show up in the way they manage their money. Men as a whole are more likely to be more aggressive with their investing dollars. They tend to think that they know more about the future direction of the financial markets than they actually do. According to a Merrill Lynch Investment Manager Survey, male investors are much more likely than women to (1) buy a hot investment without research, (2) hold losing investments too long, and (3) ignore the tax consequences of investing decisions.

Women, on the other hand, are generally more cautious in regard to investing. They tend to have better results than their male counterparts. According to a Merrill Lynch survey on investing, women are less knowledgeable about investing and less interested in investing. Yet they make fewer mistakes and do not repeat them as often. Women research their investments more thoroughly. Lastly, they aren't afraid to ask for help from a financial professional when they feel they need it. Combining the confidence that men have with the caution that the women have would provide a good chance to create an above average investor.

Besides their psychological makeup, men and women's life expectancies and work profiles are different. The average woman lives about 5 years longer than the average man. Not only do women outlive men, but also there is a much greater chance that a woman will live into her 80s. Two-thirds of people older than 85 are female.

Although this is changing, fewer women are employed full-time than men. Wage inequities exist. There are still instances today where women make less money than men even when they are doing the same job. Women also tend to have more interruptions in their career (mainly due to family obligations) and usually retire from the work force earlier than men. This is even more of a reason for women to have a handle on their finances. They should make sure they confide with a trusted person regarding their financial affairs and inform them where important legal and investment documents are located.

Married versus Single

Whether you are single or in a committed relationship can influence the way you spread out your assets. Clearly, there is more freedom for single people without dependents to do what they want with their money. They do not have to answer to anyone.

A new suit, a vacation in the Caribbean—single people can spend their money any way they see fit. Single people though should keep in mind their life goals when managing their money.

Objectives such as putting money in a retirement account and trying to buy a home should not be neglected by singles. With money not needed for important short term goals, single people can be very aggressive. They should though have an emergency fund set up in case unforeseen events occur.

Married people have to think of what is best for "we" instead of what is best for "me" in regard to the way their assets are allocated. There should be no such thing as individual investor goals in a marriage; they need to be joint goals after you tie the knot. Before the marriage vows are taken, the bride and groom should discuss their individual financial resources and what they see as their long term financial objectives as a couple. There needs to be an open dialogue about money. In committed relationships, there should be no financial secrets.

The fact that another is relying on the accumulated assets leads a partner to be more conservative than a single person. Equities, fixed income, and cash instruments should be part of the assets held by everyone regardless of marital status. All things being equal, married people should have a slightly lower weight in stocks and slightly higher weights in bonds and cash than single people. It is important that both partners participate in the investment process. One party to the marriage should not make all the financial decisions. If a financial advisor is hired, both husband and wife should meet with that person.

While health and property insurance are equally important to single and married people, life insurance is needed much more by married couples. This is especially true when one person in the relationship is not working. Remember, life insurance should be used to replace potentially lost income, not as an investment opportunity.

Novice Investor versus Experienced Investor

The difference in the way inexperienced and experienced investors manage their money is mainly their comfort level in using certain financial instruments and whether they hire a financial advisor. The lower the comfort level individuals have with investing, the more conservative they tend to be. New investors should remember that even famous investors like Warren Buffett and Peter Lynch were beginners at one time. Beginning investors often look for guidance from professionals. There is a good chance that a new investor has no idea what asset allocation is.

Carefully evaluate the credentials of all financial professionals. Check on their educational background and make sure they have appropriate work experience. See whether they have a chartered financial analyst (CFA) designation or a certified financial planner (CFP) designation, have brokerage licenses, such as the series 7 and series 63, or whether they are a certified public accountant (CPA) or an attorney. Knowing their background and credentials will help you determine their strengths and will make you better able to assess if they can help with your specific financial needs. Make sure you hire someone who is not merely a product salesperson looking to get fat commissions on proprietary products his or her firm sells, but a person who has your best financial interest at heart. Ask if you can talk to some of their clients who have similar needs to yours to see what their experience has been using the financial professional. The more questions you ask the professional up front, the fewer surprises you will encounter with future service.

Overall, get as much information you can about the services, background, and fees of any professional you hire. You want to feel confident that their advice will meet your needs, that they are credible, and above all, that the benefits of working with them justify the expense. Unfortunately, the amount people pay for financial advice compared to the value they get from it is usually completely out of whack. Before implementing anyone's advice, make sure that it is logical and makes intuitive sense.

If a beginner chooses to use a financial advisor, it is imperative that the person chosen is competent and the services provided are reasonably priced. Bottom line—if you hire someone to tend to some of your financial matters, you need to trust that they have your best interest in mind. If you do not fully trust them, do not hire them. You should also remember that there is never a bad question. If you do not understand how an investment works ask questions.

New investors are often steered to mutual funds as their investment vehicle. The diversification and the professional portfolio management they provide is the main selling point to novice investors. No-load funds with low expense ratios are the only types of funds that should be purchased.

Experienced investors are more do-it-yourselfers. Reading the business section of the newspaper and watching CNBC are part of their daily routine. They hire a brokerage firm to do physical trades, not for advice. They tend to do business with the eTrades and Charles Schwabs of the world, not the Merrill Lynchs and Smith Barneys. Experienced investors usually do not just put their money in plain-vanilla mutual and exchange-traded funds. They generally have some money allocated to individual securities. For the most part, the more experience investors have, the more comfortable with risk they are. Also, their expectations for their investment results tend to be more realistic than those of novice investors.

Dependents versus No Dependents

If you have people who are dependent on you financially, you should be more conservative with your money. If your dependents need money for something important in the short term, you should take very little risk with the assets being used to satisfy this need. Besides your children, you may have parents who you also need to help financially. You have less discretionary income when there are others who need you to provide for them. You do not want your loved ones to suffer because of bad investment choices you make. Insurance, especially life insurance, is a must for those with dependents. If your life tragically ends, you do not want your dependents to suffer financially in addition to the emotional loss.

If you do not have dependents, you can take more chances with your money. Fewer people will be impacted if your portfolio suffers losses. Your spouse, if you have one, will be the only one directly affected by your financial mistakes. Assets that can provide capital appreciation such as stocks should have a higher percentage in the portfolios of people who do not have dependents compared to those that do. Growth of capital is usually a major goal of individuals with no dependents.

Struggling Financially versus Wealthy

The more money you have, the more choices you have for your investments. For example, hedge funds require high initial investments. Also, some full-service brokerages require you to deposit a large amount to open an account and subsequently require you to keep a certain minimum balance. Many investment advisors will not talk to you unless you have a certain amount of money. Unfortunately, the amount of money you have is what a lot of the financial world uses to decide whether or not to provide you with certain products and services.

Tax-efficient investments such as municipal bonds and exchange-traded index funds offer more benefits for the wealthy. Substantial reductions in the amount you owe the IRS can be gained by having some assets in these types of products. The number that is important is not the amount of money you make on your investments, but the amount you keep.

The wealthy can take more risk with their portfolios than those with less money. As long as the money is not tied to any important short term goal, there is more wiggle room for them to position their assets. Knowing that you have a substantial amount of capital and are able to meet your financial obligations regardless of your investment results allows you to take a chance on some speculative investments. If the aggressive plays do not work out, your lifestyle will not be affected.

If you are not affluent, there are still many good investment choices available. You just need to know where to look. Money management firms with very good track records, such as Vanguard, T. Rowe Price, and Fidelity, offer a wide range of no-load funds with all sorts of strategies that require $3,000 or less to invest in. Many of these funds have reasonable expense ratios. You can buy individual stocks and bonds through discount brokerage firms at a fraction of the cost that full-service firms charge.

Low-cost, diversified funds should make up the core of the portfolio of the less wealthy. You do not need a lot of money to have exposure to all the major asset classes. Balanced funds, asset allocation funds, or a combination of equity, fixed income, and money market funds will fit the bill. You can add more asset classes and select some nonpooled securities as your wealth begins to increase.

Overall Goals for Your Portfolio

You can have numerous portfolios goals. I have narrowed them down to five general goals:

1. Capital Preservation
2. Conservative Income
3. Growth and Income
4. Growth
5. Aggressive Growth

The differences between these goals are not always black and white. These goals are discussed in detail in Part III. The risk and return potential increases progressively as you go from capital preservation to aggressive growth. The chapters that follow offer examples of portfolios and securities that can be used to satisfy each of these objectives. Most individual's assets should be managed using one or a combination of these goals. Be aware that the advantage of one of the goals often comes at the expense or benefit of another. For example, if your main desire is the safety of your principal, you must sacrifice the large return potential of a growth strategy.

Figure 8.1 can serve as a starting point for the discussion of the weights that can be assigned to asset classes for people with different goals. These percentages are a starting point, not a set-in-stone recommendation. These sample allocations just serve as a frame of reference for you to consider. You need to apply your personal circumstances to developing a portfolio. Note that the capital preservation and

Figure 8.1 Asset Allocation and Goals

	Capital Preservation	Income	Growth and Income	Growth	Aggressive Growth
Stocks	0.00%	25.00%	45.00%	60.00%	85.00%
Bonds	25.00%	45.00%	30.00%	20.00%	0.00%
Cash	75.00%	20.00%	20.00%	10.00%	0.00%
Real estate	0.00%	10.00%	5.00%	5.00%	5.00%
Commodities	0.00%	0.00%	0.00%	5.00%	10.00%

aggressive growth allocations are for those who have these as their absolute goals.

Points to Remember

- Many circumstances that you face besides the primary factors can influence how you tilt your portfolio.
- The younger you are, the more aggressive you can be with your money.
- Your money cannot increase by compounding if you have no money to compound.
- If you need money in the very short term, you should not put it in the stock market.
- Men and women often approach investing differently. Combining the confidence that men have with the caution that women have would provide a good chance to create an above average investor.
- Single people without dependents have more freedom to do what they want with their money than married people do.
- Novice and experienced investors manage their money differently depending on their comfort level using certain financial instruments and whether they seek help from a financial professional.
- If you have dependents, you will probably be more conservative with your money.
- Life insurance is a must for those with dependents.
- The more money you have, the more choices you have for your investments.

PART III

THE FIVE INVESTMENT STRATEGIES

CHAPTER 9

CAPITAL PRESERVATION

A big part of financial freedom is having your heart and mind free from worry about the what-ifs of life.

SUZE ORMAN

If you are an extremely risk averse investor, your primary objective should be capital preservation. You do not want the principal in your accounts to decline in value. Safety is your number one goal. You sacrifice high returns to keep the value of your portfolio stable. Your upside is very modest but your downside is also very modest. Capital protection, not appreciation, is your motto. Your emphasis is on the return *of* your assets, not the return *on* your assets.

You want to be able to sleep at night. You want to know with certainty that when you wake up, your portfolio will be worth exactly as much as it was when you went to sleep.

Capital preservation and liquidity go hand in hand. When you want your money, you want to be able to convert your assets into cash quickly and at a very low cost. Excluding contributions and withdrawals, there should be virtually no price difference in your portfolio with this objective from day to day and minute to minute. If you have $200,000 with this strategy today, you expect there to be at least $200,000 a week from now.

Capital preservation does come with negatives. This kind of investing comes with a high opportunity cost. Your potential returns are very small compared to any other investment style. Your returns will struggle to keep up with the pace of inflation. The percentage increase in the Consumer Price Index (CPI) from 1996 to 2006 is shown in Figure 9.1. Over time, there is a good chance the relative value of your portfolio will decline and its purchasing power will decrease if it is invested with this objective in mind. Also, when riskier assets perform well, you will not participate in any of the gains. You need to think how you will feel if you see the Standard & Poor's 500 rise 30% in a year, when you are getting only a very minimal return. There is no chance of getting rich with a strict capital preservation portfolio. There is, however, a good chance of staying rich with this type of strategy.

Most people have capital preservation as a goal for a portion of their money. Anyone with a checking account has an asset with this objective. Money that you need for everyday transactions should have the lowest risk possible attached to it. For important short term goals, whether it is to fund a college education in a few months or for a down payment on a home, you should choose accounts with safety of principal as the foremost objective.

Some people rightly or wrongly do not want to put any of their own capital at risk. Possibly in the past, they have been burned with stocks or real estate. Some think the financial markets are rigged against the little guy. Others just want to know that they will keep the money that they worked for. If you haven't invested any money in the financial markets, you can't lose any money in the financial markets.

Many people in their retirement years want to ensure their life savings are not lost or reduced for any reason except for their own withdrawals. In retirement, some worry about their portfolio plummeting due to poor investment decisions. They realize that it is unlikely they will ever get the chance to build up their assets again. There is also a segment of the

Figure 9.1 Percent Increase in Consumer Price Index, 1996–2006

Year	CPI Increase
1996	3.3%
1997	1.7%
1998	1.6%
1999	2.7%
2000	3.4%
2001	1.6%
2002	2.4%
2003	1.9%
2004	3.3%
2005	3.4%
2006	2.5%

Source: U.S. Dept. of Labor Statistics.

investing public who want to park their money in extremely conservative investments because they expect a big market decline. Others need a waiting place while they try to determine where best to deploy their assets in the near future.

You can preserve your capital in many ways. In times past and even today, some individuals think about stuffing their assets in their mattress or in a safe place in their home. The best methods maintain the value of the asset while also getting a small rate of interest. The safety of the principal is the primary goal, with the income generated being a distant secondary goal. The income generated helps combat losing ground to inflation.

Asset Choices for Capital Preservation

Cash equivalents, money market instruments, and certain short-term fixed-income securities are the best asset classes to use to preserve your capital. Cash in currency form provides the safety of not being able to decline in absolute value. The downside is that currency provides no coupon or interest potential and that inflation reduces the value of cash. There is also the problem of where you should physically store the cash. Furthermore, if you lose cash in currency form and cannot retrieve it, you are left with nothing.

You should not use equities, including preferred stocks, in a *pure* capital preservation portfolio because equities can decline in price. Just because over the long term stocks generally provide positive returns does not mean that over the short term they cannot decline in price. Any asset that can fall in value should not be included in this conservative strategy.

Certificates of deposits (CDs) and Treasury bonds are also not ideal in isolation, because if you need to withdraw them before their maturity date, you could be subject to penalty charges and capital losses. If you incorporate safer, longer maturity securities in a capital preservation strategy, you should use laddering. With this method, after you buy a series of securities with various maturities, as time passes, you replace the maturing securities with new long term securities.

It is important that the ladder you use have securities which are maturing both in the long term and short term. In this way, any liquidity concerns that arise will be mitigated. If you stay away from bonds with default risk, you will never lose a cent in principal even in bear fixed-income markets. Laddering offers a stable alternative to the wild price and yield gyrations that can occur from a single bond. An example of a ladder would be the initial purchase of 10 different Treasury instruments maturing in 10 consecutive years in the same month. Then, once a year, you buy a new 10-year Treasury bond to replace the expiring issue.

Capital Preservation with Savings Bonds

Series EE and HH savings bonds are another viable option for capital preservation. The U.S. Treasury backs them, so the loss of principal is not a concern. The Series EE are sold in amounts as low as $50, and the HH Savings Bonds are sold in $500 denominations. They both pay interest every 6 months. Both types of bonds can be redeemed before maturity. Of these two types of savings bonds, the Series EE have been more popular. Series EE bonds that are held from 6 months to 5 years earn interest of 85% of the average yield on 6-month Treasury bills. After 5 years, the rate of interest is 85% of the average yield on 5-year Treasury notes.

Capital Preservation with Money Market Mutual Funds

As an investment instrument, money market mutual funds combine the desired qualities of this strategy of preserving your principal and providing some income. They aim to keep their values steady at $1 per share with their yields changing daily, reflecting changes in short-term interest rates. These funds invest in short term debt instruments, including government paper, commercial paper, and bank certificates of deposit. Some of these funds invest exclusively in Treasury securities and others in tax-exempt securities, whereby they pass the tax benefits to shareholders. In rising interest rate environments, these investments generally perform well compared to other asset classes. Most asset classes decline in value when interest rates are climbing, not money market instruments. Furthermore, when the yield curve is flat or inverted, money market funds offer yields that are very competitive with long term bonds.

These funds come with a disclaimer such as: "An investment in the fund is not guaranteed or insured by the Federal Deposit Insurance Corporation or any other government agency. Although the fund seeks to preserve the value of your investment, it is possible to lose money by investing in the fund."

The cases where these funds have fallen below $1 per share, which is called "breaking the buck," have been extremely rare. When it happened, the sponsoring financial firm made up the difference in their customers accounts. Only invest in money market mutual funds that are no-load and do not impose any penalties on withdrawals. Also, make sure the fund allows holders to write checks against their accounts.

Capital Preservation with Money Market Accounts

Money market accounts offered by banks generally provide lower yields than money market mutual funds. They are, however, insured up to $100,000 by the Federal Deposit Insurance Corporation (FDIC) and are technically accounts in the bank. Like money market mutual funds, with money market funds you can withdraw your money at any time. They also perform well in a rising interest rate environment. The best interest rate measure to use to compare money market accounts is the annual percentage yield (APY), which is the yield you earn on a deposit in a year, incorporating the effects of compounding. Mathematically, APY is equal to 1 plus the periodic rate (expressed as a decimal) raised to the number of periods in 1 year.

Capital Preservation with Guaranteed Investment Contracts

An option that is available in many retirement programs are guaranteed investment contracts (GICs). These are contracts in which the issuer makes a commitment to provide a specific rate of interest on invested funds for a period of time. Such contracts are generally issued by insurance companies and are often used as the very conservative option in 401(k) retirement plans. A bank investment contract (BIC) is similar to a guaranteed investment contract, but it is issued by a bank. Neither product is federally insured or regulated by the federal government.

Capital Preservation with Checking and Savings Accounts

Regular checking and savings accounts are a more straightforward option. Their appeal is their convenience, easy access, and familiarity. They are good for preserving your capital because these accounts are insured for up to $100,000 by the bank where you have your checking or savings account, assuming the bank is covered by the FDIC. Usually, with checking accounts the more checks a bank allows you to write per month without being penalized, the lower the interest rate they offer. Try to avoid checking accounts with monthly service charges and minimum balance requirements. You need to read the terms of checking and savings account agreements before signing up. Many times lesser-name banks offer better deals.

With savings accounts, you do not have the option of writing checks. Many times the number of withdrawals or transfers you can make from a savings account is limited or charges are applied. You do, however, earn higher rates of interest with these accounts compared to regular checking accounts.

Capital Preservation with Mutual Funds and Exchange-Traded Funds

Lastly, there are some mutual funds (besides money market mutual funds) and exchange-traded funds you can buy in which the safety of the capital invested is the main goal. Most of these funds have as their main component short term, low-duration, highly rated fixed income instruments. With these products you have to be extremely careful that the fund you select has capital preservation as its main objective.

Remember, just because a fund has "capital preservation" or "stable asset" in its name does not mean that it is strictly following that goal. Do your due diligence on the fund and learn as much about it as you can before placing any money in it. The appropriate fund would have the characteristics of low positive returns, very low risk, and extremely low price fluctuations. Some no-load, low-cost mutual funds, which are appropriate for someone with a capital preservation objective, are listed in Figure 9.2.

Each of the next four chapters will use screens that sift through stocks, mutual funds, and exchange-traded funds to come up with securities that meet specific investment objectives. This is the only chapter without a stock screen because equities are inappropriate for a capital preservation strategy.

Screens provide a way to filter for specific securities based on investment characteristics. For example, you can easily screen for large capitalization stocks with low price/earnings ratios and high gross profit margins or for small cap growth mutual funds with strong historical performance and a portfolio manager who has been managing the fund for at least 5 years. Advisorinsight.com, zacks.com, and fidelity.com all have screeners that I would recommend.

Figure 9.2 No-Load, Low-Cost Mutual Funds for Capital Preservation

Fund	Ticker	Expense Ratio
American Century Capital Preservation	CPFXX	0.48
Fidelity Cash Reserves	FDRXX	0.43
Fidelity Government Money Market	SPAXX	0.42
Fidelity U.S. Government Reserves	FGRXX	0.35
Fidelity U.S. Treasury Money Market	FDLXX	0.57
T Rowe Price Prime Reserve	PRRXX	0.55
T Rowe Price Short Term Bond	PRWBX	0.55
T Rowe Price Tax-Exempt Money	PTEXX	0.48
T Rowe Price U.S. Treasury Money	PRTXX	0.51
TIAA-CREF Short Term Bond	TCSTX	0.31
Vanguard Prime Money Market	VMMXX	0.30
Vanguard Short Term Bond Index	VBISX	0.18
Vanguard Short Term Federal	VSGBX	0.20
Vanguard Short Term Investment	VFSTX	0.21
Vanguard Short Term Treasury Investor Shares	VFISX	0.26
Vanguard Treasury Money Market	VMPXX	0.30

Currently, there are very few exchange-traded funds that are appropriate for people with a capital preservation goal. The only two that could be used in a portfolio with this strategy is the Lehman Treasury Bill Fund (ticker symbol SHY) and the iShares Lehman 1–3 Year Credit Bond Fund (ticker symbol CSJ). Websites such as bankrate.com, money rates.com, and rateAPY.com allow you to screen for CDs, money market accounts, and savings accounts based on various characteristics, such as the yield and the minimum amount required to open an account.

Distribution of Asset Classes within Capital Preservation Strategy

A portfolio with a *pure* capital preservation objective should be dominated by cash instruments and safe fixed income securities. See Figure 9.3. Assets that offer price stability and a decent yield are the only suitable choice. Cash instruments should be the asset class that has the highest weight. Money market mutual funds are my favorite choice within the cash equivalent category if you have a capital preservation goal. They provide tremendous liquidity, they provide a yield, and there is virtually no chance of a decline in their value.

Figure 9.3 Asset Class Mix for a Capital Preservation Strategy

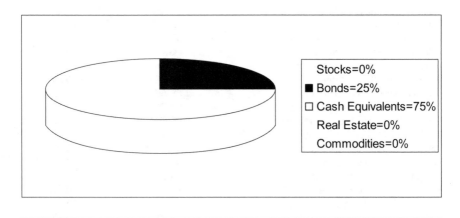

Stocks=0%
■ Bonds=25%
□ Cash Equivalents=75%
Real Estate=0%
Commodities=0%

Only highly rated corporate bonds and Treasury bonds should be the fixed income choice. Bonds offer better yields than money market instruments but they offer slightly less liquidity. It is possible to have a loss in a bond if it is sold before maturity. A Treasury bond or AAA corporate bond held until maturity will never result in a capital loss. A laddering approach, where you have a mix of highly rated short term and long term bonds, is the safest way to structure the fixed income part of your portfolio. You should choose short term bonds for a capital preservation strategy if you are forced to make a choice between short term and long term bonds.

Stocks, real estate, and commodities should not be used if you have capital preservation as your sole objective. Each of these assets provides high return potentials, but can decline in value. Any asset that is not guaranteed to maintain its value should not be held. Safety of your principal is the primary objective.

Points to Remember

- Investors whose primary objective is capital preservation are the most risk averse.
- With a capital preservation strategy, your emphasis should be on the return of your assets, not the return on your assets.
- The potential returns provided by this investing style are lower than any of the other investment styles.
- The best capital preservation methods maintain the value of the asset while also earning a small rate of interest.
- To ensure capital preservation, invest in cash equivalents, money market instruments, and certain short term fixed income securities.
- If you want to preserve your capital in the short term, do not invest in equities.

CHAPTER 10

CONSERVATIVE INCOME

The four most dangerous words in investing are: This time it's different.

SIR JOHN TEMPLETON

Investors seeking conservative income have the same main goals and priorities as investors wanting capital preservation, but the goals are in the reverse order of importance. The primary goal of individuals looking for income is investing in financial products that produce stable and relatively high amounts of cash. A high and safe yield is the ideal. Enough income should be created to offset inflation. They do not want to see a decline in the purchasing power of their assets.

The secondary goal is keeping their principal stable. Ups and downs in the value of a portfolio are tolerated as long as a sufficient amount of income is produced. They want the downside to be limited; extreme declines are not acceptable. Usually, portfolios with this goal have a low potential for significant capital appreciation.

A certain segment of the population will always have income as a main goal in their portfolio. Conservative income as an objective serves many different constituents for various reasons. The majority of investors with this goal need the actual income from their investments to live on or to help supplement their other sources of funds. Certain people want to take a lump sum of capital to create an income stream that never dips into the principal, yet provides cash for certain needs. Some believe in investing for yield as a safe way to attempt to outperform the financial markets. Others look at this style as a balance to, and a way to offset, the periodic dips in a stock-dominated portfolio.

Income from investments can be counted on much more than capital appreciation. The old adage: "a bird in the hand is worth two in the bush" applies. You can say with a much greater degree of certainty the level of income an investment will produce next year compared to what its price gain will be.

Dividends and coupons are "sticky"; firms do not want to discontinue or lower them unless they are forced to because of dire economic circumstances. When the income payout from an investment is lowered, the underlying asset usually has a precipitous drop in price. A cut in the payout is a signal to the market that the issuer is having financial problems. Corporations know this, and they try to pull out all the stops to avoid cutting their dividend.

Investments that produce more income usually involve taking more risk. Unfortunately, you do not get something for nothing in the investment world. Higher risk is the price you pay for earning a higher yield. For example, some stocks offer large yields but the chance for a decrease in their price or a cut in their dividend is extremely high. In the fixed income arena, bonds with the lowest credit ratings, and hence the highest likelihood to default and not honor their obligations, have the highest yields

In today's financial world, there is a wide range of choices with different risk and reward characteristics available for income-seeking investors. All the major asset classes offer some kind of income vehicle. You have more options than going to the bank in town that offers the highest rates on CDs. For investors, income comes in three main forms: dividends for stockholders, coupons for bondholders, and interest for holders of various cash instruments. Investors can reduce the risk of relying on income from a single security by investing in a mutual fund or exchange-traded fund that holds numerous securities and where a high and stable yield is one of its main objectives.

You also need to decide whether you want taxable income or nontaxable income. Certain investments create taxable income and others provide nontaxable income. For comparable choices, you should look at the taxable versus nontaxable yield to put each investment on equal footing. Knowing your tax bracket is essential for determining which types of income products are most appropriate.

Conservative Income with Stocks

If you want to earn a conservative return on your investments, bonds are the first assets you think of. Stocks, though, should not be ignored.

Recent legislation lowered the taxation on dividends. Under a law implemented in 2003, capital gains and dividends are taxed at the same 15% rate. Before this date, dividends were taxed at a higher rate than capital gains. More and more companies that never paid out a dividend started to and companies that already offered dividends raised them. In 2006, 900 companies in the S&P 1500 paid out some type of dividend during the year.

Many would be surprised by the amount that dividends have historically played in the overall return of stocks. Between 1926 and 2005, dividend payments accounted for over 40% of the S&P 500's total return, according to Ibbotson Associates. The yield on the S&P 500 is currently about 1.8%. There are certain sectors in the equity market which offer even higher dividend yields. Preferred stocks, along with many utilities, real estate investment trusts, and money center banks offer a substantial amount of income to their owners. Of the 10 GIC sectors in the S&P 500, currently telecommunication services, utilities, and financials offer the highest yields. Each has a dividend yield above 2.5%. The range of yields for the sectors goes from a high of 3.4% in telecommunication services and utilities to a low of 0.7% in information technology.

Conservative income investors should try to determine the safety of the yield, rather than just its size. Because a company offered a high yield the previous quarter, doesn't mean that the company will continue to offer that yield going forward. Be aware that companies that paid out a dividend the previous quarter and whose underlying stock price subsequently declined substantially will show an increase in their yield. As a result, many times in these cases the issuer announces a reduction in its dividend.

A helpful measure in determining if the dividend is safe is the dividend coverage ratio. It is calculated by dividing the trailing 12 months' operating cash flow per share by the last or expected 12 months' dividend. If the ratio is much greater than 1, an investor should feel confident that the dividend is secure. If the ratio is below 1, it means that the dividend is clearly at risk of being cut going forward. A company with a dividend coverage ratio below 1 needs to borrow or sell off assets to pay the dividend. Many companies in this position choose to reduce or forgo the dividend payment.

Standard & Poor's has a proprietary measure, the Standard & Poor's Earnings & Dividend (Quality) Ranking, that can be helpful in determining the safety of the dividend or coupon. It looks at a company's historical and current ability to generate earnings and dividends. To get a ranking, a company needs a 10-year history of earnings, a 10-year history of dividends plus the current indicated rate of its dividend, and a 2-year history of sales. The better the earnings and dividend payout history are, the higher the Quality Ranking. The rating scale for the Quality Rankings is shown in Figure 10.1. Standard & Poor's has been providing Quality Ranks since 1956.

For foreign stocks, Standard & Poor's maintains international quality rankings, IQRs. To qualify to receive an IQR, the earnings and dividend history requirement is lowered to 7 years. The growth and stability of earnings and dividends are deemed key elements in establishing S&P's earnings and dividend rankings for domestic and international stocks, which are designed to capsulize the nature of this record in a single grade.

Corporations that pay dividends are usually older and more established. They are generally not growing rapidly any more and have settled into a slower pace of expansion. Dividend payers tend to have strong balance sheets and consistent earnings growth. They have to be in a position where they can set aside a portion of their capital and distribute it to their shareholders. Instead of reinvesting their retained earnings into themselves, these mature firms tend to pay them out in the form of dividends as a way to reward shareholders. By giving the money to shareholders, there is no way for the corporation to blow the money on wasteful projects.

As noted in Chapter 9, screens provide a way to filter for specific securities based on investment characteristics. They are a tremendous source

Figure 10.1 Standard & Poor's Earnings and Dividend (Quality) Rankings

Quality Ranking	Description
A+	Highest
A	High
A–	Above average
B+	Average
B	Below average
B–	Lower
C	Lowest
D	In reorganization
NR	Not ranked

for generating investment ideas. All the screens provided in the book were run in mid 2007. Use the criteria in the screens as a helpful guide in selecting securities. Double-check to make sure the securities selected by the screen have the characteristics the screen says they do. You can do this by checking a secondary source such as Yahoo! Finance, CBSMarket watch.com, or CNBC.com. By the time you are reading this book, the actual securities selected by the screen will probably have changed.

Figures 10.2 through 10.6 show the results of a few screens that search for attractive stocks and equity mutual funds that offer high levels of income. You should do your own due diligence before placing any money in these equities. In Figures 10.2 and 10.3 all the equities are priced above $5 and have a market capitalization above a billion dollars, to avoid speculative issues. They also need to have a dividend yield greater than 4%, which is more than twice that of the S&P 500. The screen in Figure 10.2 looks for stocks with high yields and a high ranking in two proprietary Standard & Poor's measures: the equities chosen need a Quality Ranking greater than or equal to A minus and 4 or 5 STARS (*ST*ock *A*ppreciation *R*anking *S*ystem).

Figure 10.3 shows stocks with high STARS and Fair Value rankings from S&P. STARS rank stocks based on an individual analyst's opinion.

Figure 10.2 Triple Highs: High STARS, High Quality Rank, and High Yield

Price >= $5.00
Market Cap >= $1 Billion
Yield >= 4.00%
Stars >= 4
Earnings and Dividend Ranking >= A–

Ticker	Company	Dividend Yield, %	Stars	Quality Ranking
BBT	BB&T Corp	4.09	4	Above Average (A-)
BAC	Bank of America Corp	4.56	5	High (A)
C	Citigroup	4.17	5	Highest (A+)
CBL	CBL & Associates Pptys Inc	5.50	4	Above Average (A–)
DDR	Developers Rlty	5.01	5	Above Average (A-)
HCN	Health Care REIT Inc.	6.57	5	High (A)
HME	Home Properties Inc.	4.98	4	Above Average (A–)
PEI	Pennsylvania Re Invs Trust	5.13	4	Above Average (A-)
RF	Regions Financial	4.29	5	Above Average (A–)
WB	Wachovia	4.33	5	Above Average (A–)

The Fair Value rank calculates a stock's weekly Fair Value—the price at which a stock should theoretically trade at current market levels based on fundamental data such as corporate earnings and growth potential, price-to-book value, return on equity, and current yield relative to the S&P 500. Stocks are then assigned a ranking from 5, indicating that a stock's current price is significantly undervalued relative to the Fair Value universe, to 1, indicating that a stock's current price is substantially overvalued relative to the Fair Value universe.

The equities chosen need either 4 or 5 STARS and a 4 or 5 Fair Value ranking. The equities also need a high yield plus they must have increased their dividend payout 10 years in a row. Companies with a strong history of paying and increasing their dividend are more likely to continue that trend into the future. Big banks and a REIT pass the criteria of the screen.

In Figure 10.4, I searched for mutual funds that offered high yields from dividends exclusively or high yields from a combination of dividends and coupons. Few mutual fund screeners allow you to screen funds based on an equity income objective. Mutual fund screeners often have data items such as cap size, growth or value, or sectors as a way to sort out funds, but they do not usually have equity income or yield as a choice. The mutual funds in Figure 10.4 all are no-load and have expense ratios below 1. Providing decent amounts of income (with at least part of it coming from stocks) is a primary objective of the selected funds.

The iShares Dow Jones Select Dividend Fund (DVY), started in 2003, was the first exchange-traded fund targeting dividend-paying stocks. Currently, eight such ETFs are available with more coming in

Figure 10.3 Highly Rated High Dividend Stocks That Have Raised Their Dividend Payout 10 Years in a Row.

Ticker	Company	Dividend Yield, %	Stars	Fair Value Ranking	Dividend % Up Each of Last 10 Years
BAC	Bank of America Corp	4.50	5	4	100
C	Citigroup Inc	4.10	5	4	100
DDR	Developers Diversified Rlty	5.00	4	4	100
WB	Wachovia Corp	4.30	5	4	100

Figure 10.4 No-Load Mutual Funds Where Providing Income is an Objective

Fund	Ticker	Expense Ratio
Fidelity Asset Manager Income	FASIX	0.59
Fidelity Equity Income	FEQIX	0.69
Fidelity Equity Income II	FEQTX	0.68
T Rowe Price Equity Income	PRFDX	0.78
T Rowe Price Personal Strategy Income	PRSIX	0.78
Vanguard Equity Income	VEIPX	0.32
Vanguard Life Strategy Income	VASIX	0.25
Vanguard Target Retirement Income	VTINX	0.20
Vanguard Wellesley Income	VWINX	0.24

the future. The dividend ETFs are based on indexes created by four providers: Dow Jones, Mergent, Morningstar, and Standard & Poor's. There are differences between the ways these indexes are constructed. Some are weighted by market capitalization and others by dividend yield. There are also differences in the expense ratios charged. A list of the current dividend ETFs offered is displayed in Figure 10.5. Before putting money in any of them, do your own due diligence. Be aware that some of these funds also charge an additional management fee.

Foreign funds can provide decent yields as well. An investor who wants to receive income but at the same time wants the return and diversity benefits of foreign stocks should consider foreign funds. The 10 highest yielding foreign exchange-traded funds are listed in Figure 10.6. Note that some of these funds do not have a lot of assets in them. Real estate investment trusts and fixed income funds are excluded from the output.

Figure 10.5 ETFs Where Paying Dividends Is an Objective

Ticker	Index Based On	Weighted By	Expense Ratio
DVY	Dow Jones U.S. Select	Indicated Annual Yield	0.40
PFM	Mergent Broad Dividend Achievers	Modified Market Cap	0.50
PEY	Mergent Dividend Achievers 50	Yield	0.60
VIG	Vanguard Dividend Appreciation	Modified Market Cap	0.28
PHJ	Mergent High Growth Dividend Achievers	Modified Market Cap	0.50
PID	Mergent International Dividend Achievers	Yield	0.50
FDL	Morningstar Dividend Leaders	"Available Dividends"	0.45
SDY	S&P High Yield Dividend Aristocrats	Yield	0.30

Figure 10.6 Highest-Yielding Foreign ETFs* As of 6/30/07

Ticker	Name	12-Month Yield, %	Net Assets, Mil $	Expense Ratio, %
ADRD	BLDRS Developed Markets 100 ADR Index	6.44	55.0	0.3
ADRE	BLDRS Emerging Markets 50 ADR Index	5.91	266.6	0.3
KCE	streetTracks KBW Capital Markets	4.59	76.9	0.4
RSP	Rydex S&P Equal Weight	4.59	1590.0	0.4
EWM	iShares MSCI Malaysia Index	3.82	382.4	0.6
EWK	iShares MSCI Belgium Index	3.71	142.0	0.6
ADRA	BLDRS Asia 50 ADR Index	3.65	100.7	0.3
ADRU	BLDRS Europe 100 ADR Index	3.44	24.0	0.3
EPP	iShares MSCI Pacific ex-Japan	3.41	2060.0	0.5
EWS	iShares MSCI Singapore Index	3.30	585.0	0.6

*Excluding bond ETFs and REIT portfolios

Conservative Income with Bonds

All types of bonds offer income potential except for zero coupon bonds. Fixed-income securities run the gamut from Treasury bonds that offer low yields with very little risk to high-yield (junk) bonds that offer outsized yields with extremely high levels of risk. An issuer's credit rating is the primary way that the safety of the coupon payment is measured.

The credit rating shows a company's ability to pay off its debt obligations. This opinion focuses on the borrower's capacity and willingness to meet its financial commitments when they come due. Simply said, a firm that is secure making its interest payments is in better shape to pay its dividend or coupon. Standard & Poor's, Moody's, and Fitch provide credit rankings on various financial issues. The higher the current credit rating, the more secure the future income stream.

You should look at the difference between short term and long term yields and the yields of high credit-quality and low credit-quality debt. When the spreads between these issues are small, it is better to pick the shorter term, high credit-quality bonds. The higher the spreads become, the more the longer-maturity and lower-quality bonds become enticing. If you take more risk, you want to be compensated for it.

Unlike stocks, there are bonds that offer the benefit of tax-free income. Municipal bonds are triple-tax-free. They are not subject to federal, state, or local taxes. For residents in states with high taxes and for people at high-income levels, Municipal bonds can be a good option.

Backed by the full faith and credit of the U.S. government, Treasury bills, notes, and bonds are the safest of all fixed income securities. The chance of default is extremely low. You can be confident that you will receive your coupon payments and your principal back from your investment if you hold it to maturity. The government has the power and is in the enviable position of being able to raise taxes or print money to pay off their loans if times get tough.

Unlike Treasury issues, corporate bonds run the gamut from high quality to very speculative. Blue chip companies such as Johnson & Johnson and General Electric have bonds with the highest credit rating. These bonds have very little risk of default but offer low comparative returns to other corporate bonds. Most corporations, however, have less than stellar balance sheets and hence the debt they offer has lower credit ratings.

If you want to invest in more speculative bond issues, you are better off doing it in a bond mutual fund that invests in low credit-quality bonds. A mutual fund provides professional management and allows you to avoid single security risk by diversifying into several bonds. If a few bonds default, other bonds in the fund could offset their losses. Most funds do not require as much of a cash outlay as most individual bonds. A negative of bond mutual funds is that there is no set-in-stone yield and maturity date as there is with a single bond issue. Periodically, mutual funds do give information on their average yield and the duration of the overall portfolio of bonds that they hold.

Conservative Income with Cash Equivalents

Cash equivalents are the safest and most liquid of all the major asset classes that pay income to their investors. There are no speculative money market instruments or junk cash equivalents. The risk of default or loss of principal for this asset class is extremely low. Most banks offer checking, savings, and money market accounts that are insured by the FDIC up to a certain amount.

The prevailing interest rate is the main determinant of the return provided by cash equivalents. In low interest rate environments, the returns for this asset class are paltry. In high and rising interest rate environments, they usually provide high relative returns compared to the other major asset classes. Stocks and bonds generally struggle when interest rates are high and rising.

As a general rule within cash equivalents, the lower the liquidity, the higher the yield. The more time it takes you to get access to your money, without charges and penalties, the more you are rewarded. On a given date, a 1-year certificate of deposit has a higher yield than a 30-day CD at the same bank. Cash-in-hand, the most liquid of assets, earns no interest. The highest-yielding cash equivalents are the longer-term certificates of deposit. The longest term CDs offered by banks are usually for 5 years. The negative with CDs is that if you withdraw the money before the maturity, there is a penalty charge. If you do not want to take the penalty charge, your money is locked in for the term of the CD.

Conservative Income with Annuities

Another option available to people looking for income is annuities. An annuity is a contract between you and a financial firm, usually an insurance company, which requires you to make a lump-sum payment or series of payments to the financial firm. In exchange, the financial company agrees to make periodic payments to you. These annuities can provide a steady stream of income that can help you reduce the risk of outliving your assets. Annuities can offer income immediately or the income can be deferred. With deferred annuities the income stream doesn't begin until a certain value has been accumulated through prior premium payments or after a certain amount of time has passed. For example, you may not get your income payments until you have deposited $100,000 or 5 years has elapsed.

Annuities provide income that is guaranteed to last as long as you live or your spouse lives. The only caveat is the claims-paying ability of the issuing insurance company, which means that if the company goes out of business, you are out of luck. Financial firms typically offer tax-deferred growth of earnings and may include a death benefit that will pay your beneficiary a guaranteed minimum amount. Similar to traditional IRAs, annuity income is fully taxed when it is withdrawn. Furthermore, there are steep surrender charges if you want early access to your principal.

What's the difference between fixed and variable annuities? Fixed annuities guarantee a certain payment amount just like a fixed-rate mortgage charges a fixed interest rate. Variable annuities do not make such a guarantee, but offer the potential for greater returns. Variable annuities are like variable rate mortgages, where the interest rate you pay can go up if interest rates go up. For a variable annuity, the amount of the periodic payments you receive will vary depending on the performance of the investment options you have chosen. For example, many people invest their variable annuities in equity mutual funds, which can have volatile performance over different time periods. Variable annuities come with disclaimers: for example, "Principal values and investment returns will fluctuate, and you may have a gain or loss when money is received."

Equity-indexed annuities are a hybrid between fixed and variable rate annuities. They pay a minimum rate of interest but also give you the chance to participate in the gains of the stock market. The insurer usually guarantees a minimum return, which is based on changes in an equity index, such as the S&P 500. Once the accumulation period has ended, the investor receives periodic payments or a lump sum from the insurer.

Be aware that annuities can carry very costly fees. The charges on these products have been notoriously high, to the point of wiping out their value to consumers. Many variable annuities have sales commissions of around 5% and have ongoing management fees of more than 2% per year.

Another problem is the overly aggressive techniques salesmen use to sell annuities, which are not always on the up-and-up. Annuity sales tactics have historically been on the top of regulators' lists of scams and scandals. Overall, highly rated tax-free bonds are a better option than fixed rate annuities, because of their lower cost and lower default risk. And no-load mutual funds are a better choice than variable annuities because of their lower cost and the diversification benefits they provide. In almost all cases, if you want income, annuities are probably not your best choice.

Distribution of Asset Classes within Conservative Income Strategy

If you have conservative income as your goal, there are numerous asset classes to choose from. Your primary goal is a stable amount of income,

Figure 10.7 Asset Mix for Conservative Income Strategy

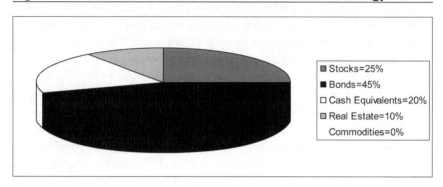

- Stocks=25%
- Bonds=45%
- Cash Equivalents=20%
- Real Estate=10%
- Commodities=0%

and your secondary goal is price stability. Bonds should have the highest weight in your portfolio. They offer the best combination of high yields and price stability. Long term bonds can make up a higher weight in your portfolio than if you have a capital preservation objective because liquidity is less of a concern. Figure 10.7 shows an appropriate conservative asset mix.

Cash instruments and equities should be present in this strategy, but they do come with some weaknesses. Cash instruments offer more stability but a lower yield than bonds. Stocks, including real estate investment trusts, can offer high yields but can decline in price. Having a diverse group of asset classes lowers the volatility of the funds you have targeted with a conservative income strategy.

Points to Remember

- If you are seeking income, your primary goal is investing in financial products that produce stable and relatively high amounts of cash.
- If you are an investor who seeks conservative income, you probably need the actual income from your investments to live on or to help supplement your other sources of funds.
- You can count on income from your investments much more than capital appreciation.

- Firms do not want to discontinue or lower dividends unless they are forced to by dire economic circumstances.
- Higher risk is the price you pay for earning a higher yield.
- A disadvantage of bond mutual funds is that there is no set-in-stone yield or maturity date like you have with a single bond issue.
- Annuities are not the best choice for generating income.

CHAPTER 11

GROWTH AND INCOME

You can't escape the responsibility of tomorrow by evading it today.
ABRAHAM LINCOLN

If you need income from your portfolio and you want a little more juice from your investments than a standard income-oriented portfolio can deliver, growth and income should be your objective. Investors who want to combine income with growth are looking to get the best of both worlds—capital appreciation and a decent yield from their portfolio. People with this objective should expect a combination of capital appreciation and income from their portfolio. But they should expect less of a yield than someone with an income objective and less growth than someone with a growth objective. Ideally, they would like their portfolio to consistently increase in size and provide a yield that outpaces inflation. The strategy is a way to take part in stock market gains while protecting somewhat against downside risks.

Be aware that you can lose money with a growth and income strategy. Although unlikely, you might lose over 20% in a severe bear market if you seek growth and income. The more you weight your portfolio toward common stocks, the more likely that you will suffer a sharp decline.

Typically, investors with a growth and income objective will have intermediate to long time horizons for their investable assets. Since there is a chance of short term losses, a minimum time horizon of three years is recommended. This strategy is not appropriate for individuals who will need their principal in the very near future.

Many different kinds of people are seeking growth and income. Retirees who are trying to combat inflation and want more than just income from their savings choose this strategy. Some conservative investors who are willing to give up some potential return for a lower level of risk sometimes pick a growth and income objective. Others believe that ignoring the income-generating potential of securities is not a way to beat the market considering how much fixed income yields can contribute to their overall total return. Furthermore, income is more consistently returned by investments than capital gains. You can have a pretty good estimate of the income a security will produce; the price appreciation generated in the future is merely a guess.

Growth and income are not mutually exclusive aspects for an investable security. You will need to make some sacrifices if you want to obtain both goals. If you want to get capital appreciation of 50% and a 10% yield in a year, you might want to lower your expectations. A growth and income strategy should be viewed as more conservative than a "pure" growth portfolio and more aggressive than a "pure" income portfolio. A moderate amount of income with a moderate amount of capital gains should be your expectation. The higher the amount an investment offers of appreciation and yield, the greater the risk that the goals will not be achieved.

You can take a few different approaches. You can buy individual securities and funds that offer the potential for capital appreciation and a yield. Another strategy is that you can combine a mix of securities, where some offer the chance for capital appreciation and others offer income potential exclusively. Others who are comfortable using derivatives can invest in attractively priced stocks and earn current income by selling covered call options on their portfolio of stocks.

Growth and Income with Real Estate

Owning real estate can achieve your growth and income objectives. You can buy a property and collect rental income from it. If the property increases in value, you stand a chance of receiving capital appreciation when it is sold.

However, physical real estate is not a very liquid asset, meaning it can be tough to sell. It takes some time for a real estate transaction to culminate. You also have to act as a landlord for the property you own. You are responsible for collecting the rent and repairing the wear and tear of the property. In many cases the property owner contracts out for someone to handle these types of tasks.

Growth and Income with Stocks

Stocks as an asset class offer the opportunity for growth and income. Equities over the long term have provided capital appreciation of 8% and a dividend yield of 3% annually. To provide both objectives of this strategy on a consistent basis, an individual stock clearly needs strong financials. Creating solid earnings and cash flow numbers per share over time are a must. The company needs to have enough money to pay out dividends to shareholders and have some left aside to invest in the underlying business.

Most stocks that offer the opportunities for growth and income are well established, having been in business for a number of years, and have reached a large size which is represented by a sizable market capitalization. The sectors of the equity market that offer the most choices are financial companies, real estate investment trusts, utilities, and telecom companies. The best choices are companies that have consistently grown their earnings and have year after year raised their dividends. Companies that have done this have proven that during good times and bad times they can return money to their shareholders. A consistently rising dividend reveals the profitable progress of a company.

Being able to provide capital appreciation does not mean that the equity has to be a "growth" stock with a high price to earnings ratio, high growth rate, and high price to book multiple. The stock could be a value stock or any classification of stock that offers the potential for capital appreciation. Remember, growth of capital is the objective no matter how it is achieved. Many times stocks that have been beaten down in the market but whose dividend paying abilities remain intact offer the best growth and income opportunities. The stock may be attractively valued, it may offer the chance of increasing sales and profit margins, or it may be seeing strong demand from consumers. The important aspect is that the stock offers a good chance of being priced higher in the future than it is today.

The stock screens in Figures 11.1 and 11.2 display equities that can provide capital appreciation and a reasonable yield. Stocks which have projected annual earnings per share growth rates above 7% and have raised their earnings per share each of the past 5 years are filtered for in Figure 11.1. To satisfy the income requirement of the strategy each of the stocks needs to yield above 2.5%, which is greater than the yield of the S&P 500. The yield of the S&P 500 currently stands at about 1.8%.

Stocks that have a PEG ratio less than 1.3 and a dividend yield above 3% are outputted in Figure 11.2. Stocks with PEG ratios below 1.3 appear attractively valued, whereby their projected growth rate is low compared to the valuation being put on their earnings. Each of the selections also has an S&P Earnings & Dividend Rank of B+ or above, which shows that the earnings and dividends have been relatively stable over the long term. In each of the screens the selected stocks have at least a 4 STARS rating (Buy) from S&P analysts and meet minimum price and market cap requirements.

Growth and Income with Bonds and Money Market Instruments

Most individual fixed income and money market securities are not suited for the growth and income strategy. They fulfill the income part of the equation easily, but struggle with the growth part. Most bonds

Figure 11.1 Highly Rated Growth and Income Stocks As of 6/30/07

Market Cap >= $1 Billion
Yield >= 2.5%
Stars >= 4
EPS Projected 5-Year Growth >= 7
EPS % Up Last 5 Years = 100%

Ticker	Company	Dividend Yield	Stars	EPS Projected Growth Rate	EPS % Up Last 5 Years = 100%
BAC	Bank of America	4.5	5	7.58	100%
CFR	Cullen/Frost Bankers	3.0	5	9.67	100%
GE	General Electric	2.9	5	10.56	100%
JNJ	Johnson & Johnson	2.7	4	8.31	100%
MI	Marshall & Ilsley Corp.	2.6	4	9.42	100%
MCHP	Microchip Technology, Inc.	3.0	4	16.00	100%
SNV	Synovus	2.6	4	12.14	100%
TOT	Total S.A.	2.6	4	7.00	100%
UGI	UGI Corp.	2.7	4	8.00	100%
WB	Wachovia Corp.	4.3	4	8.88	100%

Figure 11.2 Stocks with Attractive Valuations Combined with a High Yield As of 6/30/07

Price >= $5.00
Market Cap >= $500 Million
Yield >= 3.00%
Stars >= 4
S&P Earnings and Dividends Ranking >= B+
PEG Ratio <= 1.3

Ticker	Company	Dividend Yield	Stars	Earnings and Dividend Rank	PEG Ratio
C	Citigroup	4.17	5	A+	1.2
FR	First Ind. Rlty.	4.33	4	B+	0.9
FRE	Freddie Mac	3.29	4	A	1.1
WB	Wachovia	4.33	4	A–	1.2

and cash equivalents do not provide the chance for significant capital appreciation. The day-to-day prices of these instruments do not move very much. Bonds that are purchased at a discount offer the chance for some (usually small amounts) of capital appreciation if they are held to term. A bond purchased at par that is held to maturity does not offer the opportunity for the growth of capital. If it is sold before maturity, there is the chance for capital appreciation if it is sold for more than its purchase price. As long as it is not a zero coupon bond and is in good financial condition, there will always be an income component for a fixed income security. The income is generally provided in steady payments until the bond reaches its maturity date.

Out of the main types of bonds, corporates provide the best opportunity for capital appreciation and yield. Among the different classifications of fixed income securities, they offer the highest yield. Low-credit-grade corporates offer the best yield in the bond universe. Corporates also are the least likely to be purchased at par. When sold before maturity, they provide the opportunity for some capital appreciation. Credit upgrades, good earnings results, and an improving business environment can raise the price of a corporate bond.

Convertible bonds, a special type of corporate bond, offer a growth and income opportunity because they pay a specific interest rate but also give the holder the right to convert the bonds into a given number of shares of common stock. In tough times, unless the company goes bankrupt, holders will get their coupon payments. If the issuing company hits it big, the convertible bondholders will profit along with the other stockholders.

Convertible bond mutual funds are a better choice than individual convertible issues. Convertible funds provide diversification, low initial investments, and professional management. A collection of convertible bonds is more likely to achieve a growth and income objective than an individual issue. The Vanguard Convertible Securities Fund (VCVSX) is an example of a mutual fund that is primarily made up of convertibles; it has provided good returns and it has low expenses.

The majority of investors use mutual funds and exchange-traded funds to achieve their growth and income objective. Many balanced funds are appropriate. They typically have a mix of equity, fixed income, and cash instruments in their portfolios. There are also many funds that have "growth and income" in their title or as their objective. Before investing in these funds, read the prospectus and investigate to make sure they actually are what they say they are. In the mutual fund world: You cannot always judge a book by its cover. Make sure that one of the mandates of the fund is to try to produce *both* capital gains and a decent yield. Figure 11.3 screens for balanced mutual funds that have many qualities you would want if you have a growth and income objective.

A vehicle that pools securities offers a greater chance that both needs will be satisfied. If a single security in a fund falls in price or reduces its yield, it could be made up by other stocks or bonds in the fund. Individual securities have a greater chance of failing to achieve one of the goals. Funds that are classified as balanced, equity income, growth and income, and dividend growth can provide capital appreciation and a decent yield. In most cases, the yield part of the equation is easier to achieve. The more difficult part is providing capital appreciation, especially when the overall stock market is declining.

Distribution of Asset Classes within the Growth and Income Strategy

If you have a growth and income objective, stocks should have the highest weight. They offer the best opportunity for capital appreciation

Figure 11.3 Attractive Balanced Funds

Search Criteria
  Fund Group=Balanced
  Manager Tenure>=5 years
  No Load Funds Only
  Expense Ratio<=1.00%
  Morningstar Rating= 4 or 5 stars
  1 year Return>= category average
  3 year Return>= category average
  5 year Return>= category average

Output

Ticker	Fund Name	Morningstar Rating	Expense Ratio
ADBAX	Advance Capital I Balance	4 Stars	0.93
CAIBX	American Funds Capital Income Builder	4 Stars	0.55
MMAIX	MFS Moderate Allocation I	4 Stars	0.87
OAKBX	Oakmark Equity & Income	5 Stars	0.86
RPBAX	T. Rowe Price Balanced	4 Stars	0.64

combined with a decent yield. Over the long term, equities have consistently outpaced inflation. A growth and income strategy (see Figure 11.4) should be tilted toward large capitalization stocks that have strong financials and have consistently paid a dividend.

Bonds and cash instruments provide a yield but minimal capital appreciation potential. Their job in the portfolio is to produce income,

Figure 11.4 Asset Mix for Growth and Income Strategy

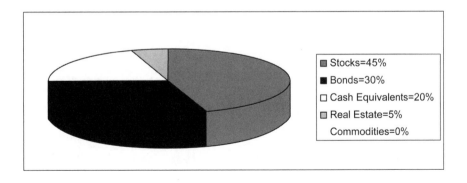

- Stocks=45%
- Bonds=30%
- Cash Equivalents=20%
- Real Estate=5%
  Commodities=0%

some price stability, and diversification benefits. Real estate also provides growth and income potential. Real estate investment trusts (REITs) provide the least expensive and most liquid way to gain real estate exposure.

Points to Remember

- If your objective is growth and income, you ideally want a portfolio that consistently increases in size and provides a yield that outpaces inflation.
- Since you run the risk of short-term losses with a growth and income objective, your minimum time horizon should be three years.
- The higher the return your investment offers, the greater the risk that you will not achieve it. This applies to both capital appreciation and yield.
- To achieve growth and income, you can either buy individual securities or funds that offer the potential for providing both growth and income. Or you can combine a mix of securities where some securities just offer capital appreciation potential and others just offer income potential.
- Stocks of financial companies, REITs, utilities, and telecom companies offer the most choices for growth and income investments.
- Corporate bonds provide the best opportunity for capital appreciation and yield in the fixed income universe.

CHAPTER 12

GROWTH

Take calculated risks. That is quite different from being rash.

GEORGE S. PATTON

Many investors want their portfolios to grow. Simply put, they want the value of their investments to increase and substantially beat the inflation rate. They want to be able to afford in tomorrow's dollars what they cannot afford in today's dollars. The main lore of the financial markets—especially the stock market—is that they provide the opportunity for you to substantially increase your wealth.

However, most asset classes cannot even beat the inflation rate. For your investments to break even, they must appreciate at least as much as the rate of inflation. Since 1960, the cost of living has risen about 4% a year. At this rate more than half of your portfolio's buying power would be lost in less than 20 years if it did not earn a return.

Many choose a growth strategy to achieve their long-term objectives. The time frame for portfolios with this goal should be 5 years or longer. If you need to use your money in less than 5 years, a growth strategy is inappropriate because there is a chance you will lose money.

If you want to employ a growth strategy, make sure you have a long time horizon for your money. An attractive aspect of a long term approach to investing in financial assets is that it reduces day-to-day risk and worry. A sharp decline in a single period has plenty of time to be made up.

Growth strategies are often ideal for people in their early or middle career years who are interested in building their long term wealth. They want good yearly results to compound into good long term performance. They accept that there will be years when they lose money. These periods, however, should be more than offset by the periods with strong positive performance.

A growth strategy is usually employed in the early funding years for important goals that can be a long way off, such as retirement and paying for a child's tuition. The hope is that strong performance in the early years will compound into a sizable amount of money for when it will be ultimately needed. As the target date approaches, the growth goal should shift into a more conservative mode. This usually involves lowering the amount of equities and raising the weighting of safer fixed income and money market instruments. You do not want to make the mistake of having the assets that you have built up over a number of years subject to a sharp market decline right before they are needed.

A growth strategy has some risk attached to it. This can be tempered by your time horizon: the longer your time period, the lower your risk. The growth strategy is more risky than growth and income and less risky than aggressive growth. Do not expect to earn a high yield from a growth portfolio. The vast majority of the gains will come from capital appreciation. There is not the safety net of a lot of income being produced from dividends and coupons to mitigate your losses during a market downturn.

Growth with Equities

The main asset class that will be used to achieve growth is equities. Most people are drawn to equities because of the growth of capital potential they can provide despite their unpredictable future. Attractive valuations, increasing earnings, and positive business developments all can lead to gains in a stock going forward. Over long periods of time, stocks are the best performing of the major asset classes and the only one to significantly outpace inflation.

A stock does not necessarily have to be a classic growth stock to provide capital appreciation. With the growth strategy, the dividend yield and the ability of the company to pay the dividend is of little importance. The goal is to select equities that provide the potential for capital appreciation regardless of whether they are considered growth or value stocks. In bull markets, the growth strategy will outperform most other strategies. Be aware though that in bear markets they will be much harder hit than the other strategies. Even great companies with cheap stock prices can have big declines in price because of macroeconomic factors outside of their control. The Federal Reserve unexpectedly raising interest rates, a war breaking out, and a severe weather event are examples of actions that can come with little warning and that can lead to sharply lower stock prices.

The main equity investing philosophies are growth, value, and GARP (growth at a reasonable price). Those who employ the growth style look for companies that are growing faster than the market. Their valuation ratios, such as the price/earnings, price/book, and price/sales, are higher than the average company. The hope of the growth investor is that the growth will continue and lead to a sharp appreciation in the stock. Information technology and biotechnology have been historically well represented in the growth category.

Figure 12.1 is a screen for growth stocks. Each of the stocks is in the highest quintile of the stock universe in terms of its projected 5-year earnings per share (EPS) growth and EPS growth projected next year versus this year. To qualify, the minimum 5-year EPS growth rate turned out to be 28% and the minimum EPS growth projected next year versus this year was 56%. Also, to be selected each of the stocks needs to have a gross profit margin over 50% (the market median for the U.S. equity market is a gross profit margin of 38.1%) and has to be highly regarded by Standard & Poor's equity analysts, having a 4 or 5 STARS ranking. Lastly, each stock needs to have a price above $5 and a market cap above a billion dollars, to avoid speculative issues. The companies that are returned by this screen have many of the characteristics a growth investor is looking for.

Value investors try to find companies that have the opposite characteristics of the growth companies. They believe value companies are worth more than what they are trading for; the assumption being that the stocks will appreciate when the market ultimately recognizes their value. Value companies are slow growing and often in old-line industries. These companies often have had recent price declines and do not draw a lot of attention from the typical investor. Value investors believe that the market is underestimating the prospects for the company. Since these stocks are cheap, any positive surprise can lead to big gains. The art of successful value investing is distinguishing between stocks that are cheap because the market is overlooking something and stocks that are cheap because their future prospects are bleak.

Figure 12.1 Growth Stock Screen As of 6/30/07

Search Criteria

	Low Value	High Value
Traded on U.S. Exchanges		
Price of Stock	$5	
Market Cap	$1 billion	
EPS Growth (Projected 5-Year) Highest 20%	28.00%	
EPS Growth (Projected Next Year vs. This Year) Highest 20%	56.00%	
Gross Profit Margin	50.00%	
S&P Stars	4	5

Output

Symbol	Company	Price of Stock	Market Cap in Millions	EPS Growth Projected Next vs. This Year	EPS Growth Projected 5 Years	Gross Profit Margin	S&P Stars Rank
AMT	Amer. Tower CP	42.00	17,500	107.4	48.3	74.1	4
CELG	Celgene Corporation	57.33	22,000	61.2	48.3	91.0	4
DO	Diamond Offshore Drilling	101.56	14,000	63.0	28.0	58.7	4
KYPH	Kyphon	48.15	2,200	56.8	33.3	90.9	4

In Figure 12.2 the screen filters for value stocks by looking for companies that have a price to earnings ratio in the lowest quintile of the entire stock universe. This works out to their having a P/E below 14 to qualify. Each stock selected also has to have a dividend yield above 3% and a Standard & Poor's Earnings and Dividend Ranking of A or better. A minimum $5 stock price and $5 billion dollars in market cap are also required to be selected. The companies found by the screen turn out to be only financials. If you lower the market cap requirement to $1 billion some REITS are outputted.

Growth at a reasonable price (GARP) combines characteristics of both the growth and value style. It reduces the weaknesses that these individual styles have. GARP investors look for stocks that are growing faster than the market but are attractively priced. The negative of the growth strategy is that you are buying stocks that are richly priced, and the negative of the value style is that you are buying stocks that are cheap because they have no growth prospects. A financial ratio that is a good measure that GARP investors use to find stock candidates is the forward price/earnings to growth rate (PEG). The PEG divides the price/earnings ratio by its estimated future growth rate. Stocks with a PEG between 0 and 1 are generally viewed as good candidates for GARP investors. You should compare the PEG ratio of a company to the ratio of its competitors and to the sector it is in as a whole.

When you are examining a PEG, try to determine how many analysts' forecasts went into the predicted growth rate. Analysts covering the company provide the future growth rate estimates. When fewer than three analysts participate, the number given for the growth rate is not very meaningful. The predictions of one or two analysts are too small of a sample for a useful financial ratio.

The screen in Figure 12.3 searches for stocks that are growing at a reasonable price. Each stock has a PEG ratio of 1 or below with at least five Wall Street analysts providing coverage. Each has a debt to capital ratio in the lowest quintile of the stock universe and a 4 or 5 STAR rating from Standard & Poor's equity analysts. Like many of the other screens, a minimum of a $5 stock price and a billion dollars in market capitalization are required.

All three of these investment philosophies provide the opportunity for growth of capital for the equities in your portfolio. Of the investing styles, growth tends to outperform in bull markets, while value generally

Figure 12.2 Value Stock Screen As of 6/30/07

Search Criteria	Low Value	High Value
Traded on U.S. Exchanges		
Price of Stock	$5	
Market Cap	$5 Billion	
Dividend Yield	3.00%	
P/E This Year Lowest Quintile		14%
S&P Earnings and Dividend Rank	A	

Output

Symbol	Company	Market Cap in Millions	Dividend Yield	P/E	Estimated This Year S&P Earnings and Dividend Rank
BAC	Bank of America	219,900	4.52	11.8	A
C	Citigroup	256,500	4.17	11.6	A+
CMA	Comerica Inc.	9,500	4.20	12.3	A
NCC	Natl. City CP	33,500	4.61	13.8	A
UB	Union Bancal CP	60,300	3.44	13.4	A
WM	Washington Mutual	38,800	5.04	11.8	A
WFC	Wells Fargo	119,200	3.14	13.10	A

Figure 12.3 GARP Stock Screen

Search Criteria

Search Criteria	Low Value	High Value
U.S. Markets		
Price of Stock	$5	
Market Cap	$1 Billion	
Peg Ratio		1
Analyst Coverage Current Qtr	5	
S&P Stars Rank	4	5
Debt to Capital (Lowest 20%)		

Output

Symbol	Company	Price of Stock*	Market Cap in Millions	Peg Ratio	Current Qtr. Analyst Coverage	S&P STARS Rank	Debt/ Capital
ANF	Abercrombie & Fitch	73.64	6,300	0.80	20	5.00	0
AEO	American Eagle Outfitters	25.72	5,600	0.80	21	4.00	0
FMCN	Focus Media Holdings Limited Sponsored ADR	47.72	5,300	0.80	17	4.00	0
GS	Goldman Sachs	221.32	91,113	0.80	18	5.00	0
OXPS	Options Xpress Holdings Inc.	25.79	1,600	0.70	7	4.00	0

*As of. 7/5/07

does the best in bear markets relative to the other strategies. Be aware that sometimes sectors that you would think would be classified a certain way are not. For example, currently most consumer staple stocks are classified as growth and most telecommunication stocks are classified as value.

You should do your homework before you buy a stock to increase your chance of getting capital appreciation. A well-researched and informed decision cannot guarantee investment success but it certainly can increase your odds. You should try to read the latest annual report and listen to the most recent analyst conference call. This information is available on the Internet on the company's home page at the Investor Relations tab. Free websites such as Yahoo! Finance allow you to look at the financial statistics of companies in a specific industry. You should compare the company's financial ratios with those of its competitors. Statistics such as the company's growth rate, price/earnings ratio, and gross profit margin are very relevant. You want to see how a company stacks up against its peers. Also, certain metrics are very important in particular industries. For example, same store sales are an important metric for retailers and revenue per room is an important measure for hotels.

Buy stocks of companies whose business you believe will improve over the next 5 years. A hot new product, getting customers and market share from a struggling competitor, and new and improved management may all be catalysts for a rising stock price. When you purchase a stock have the intent of holding it for the long term; do not buy a stock thinking it will be a short term trade.

After the decision is made to buy a stock, you should have a good idea at what price point you would sell it. You should establish two price points: one above the initial purchase price and one below the initial purchase price (hopefully, you will not have to sell at this price). It is important to have a plan for the stock before you purchase it because this will take some of the emotional aspects out of the trade. Many times greed and fear get in the way of prudent financial decisions.

If you are uncomfortable doing financial research yourself, you should get assistance from analysts through your brokerage firm. Most full-service brokerage firms have their own research analysts on staff, while most discount brokerage firms provide research from independent providers. Before taking the advice of any analyst, make sure that the analyst and the firm have no conflicts of interest with the company they are recommending. Ascertain how long the analyst has been covering the company. Lastly, get at least one second opinion. The opinions may conflict but use your judgment about which analyst makes the better case.

You should not just limit yourself to domestic stocks. International stocks can provide solid returns. Over the past 20 years, the U.S. market has not been the top-performing developed stock market in any single year (see Figure 12.4). Foreign stocks offer diversification and exposure to many economies that are growing faster than the U.S. economy. Even with the globalization of markets, most foreign companies are exposed to different business cycles and are working off smaller bases than U.S. companies. However, be aware that foreign stocks also have currency, liquidity, and political concerns tacked on to the same risks that domestic stocks carry.

Every portfolio that has growth as a goal should have some exposure to international stocks. The best way to purchase international equities

Figure 12.4 U.S. Stock Market Performance Compared to Other Developed Markets

Year	Best-Performing Developed Market	U.S. Equity Market Ranking Compared to 10 Major Markets*
1986	Japan	9
1987	Japan	6
1988	France	7
1989	Germany	4
1990	U.K.	4
1991	Hong Kong	3
1992	Hong Kong	3
1993	Hong Kong	10
1994	Japan	6
1995	Switzerland	2
1996	Hong Kong	5
1997	Switzerland	2
1998	France	3
1999	Japan	5
2000	Switzerland	7
2001	Australia	2
2002	Australia	9
2003	Germany	10
2004	Italy	10
2005	Canada	9

*1 = Highest, 10 = Lowest
Sources: Morgan Stanley Capital International, Rimes Online

is through a mutual fund or exchange-traded fund. These funds provide diversity and liquidity and, in the case of actively managed mutual funds, you get the benefit of professional portfolio management. There are many funds available that have expense ratios below 1%. An expense ratio below 1.5% is reasonable for an international fund.

Growth with Bonds and Money Market Instruments

Bonds and money market instruments are geared more for conservative income-oriented investors than for growth investors. The capital appreciation they offer is limited. Investors in these asset classes focus more on the level and reliability of their yield than they do the minimal price gains they can provide. Most people look to bonds and cash instruments for the income they offer and as a low risk alternative to stocks. Growth of capital is not an appropriate objective for fixed income and cash investments.

Growth with Real Estate and Commodities

Commodities and real estate in their physical form and as the cornerstone to a financial instrument can provide growth potential. Over the past few years there were periods where a lot of money was made within these asset classes. The major concern with both these asset classes is that the physical assets have high carrying costs and provide poor liquidity.

For commodities, there are the storage and insurance costs for holding the assets. It is wise to protect valuable commodities, such as gold and platinum from loss or theft. In the case of real estate, there are the taxes, insurance, and general upkeep costs that can put a dent in your wallet. With both asset classes, the transaction costs of buying and selling are steep and it takes longer to consummate a trade than with other asset classes.

Mutual funds and exchange-traded funds are a smart and efficient way to get exposure to real estate and commodities. They provide a way to invest in several different real estate properties and commodities.

Figure 12.5 Asset Mix for Growth Strategy

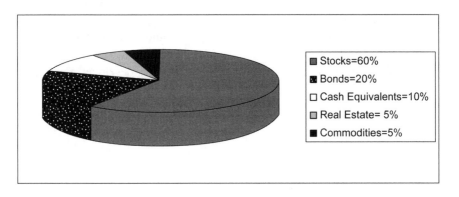

Real estate investment trusts (REITs) are the main securities that comprise real estate funds.

Distribution of Asset Classes within Growth Strategy

Stocks should be your largest asset class if you have a growth objective. The main draw of equities is their capital appreciation potential over time. In the long run, equities have outperformed all the other asset classes. International equities should make up a portion of the equity exposure. Bonds and cash are part of the portfolio to offset some of the risk of the equities. Real estate and commodities are included because they have growth potential and are not highly correlated with stocks.

Points to Remember

- The main lure of the stock market is that it provides the opportunity for you to substantially grow your wealth.
- The time frame for portfolios with a growth goal should be 5 years or longer.

- Stocks are the main asset used to achieve growth.
- A stock does not have to be a classic growth stock to provide capital appreciation.
- Every portfolio that has growth as a goal should have some exposure to international stocks.
- The U.S. market has not been the top-performing developed country stock market in any single year over the past 20 years.

CHAPTER 13

AGGRESSIVE GROWTH

October. This is one of the particularly dangerous months to speculate in stocks. Others are November, December, January, February, March, April, May, June, July, August, and September.

MARK TWAIN

In baseball, most batters would be thrilled to make solid contact with the ball and get on base three out of every ten at-bats. A few ballplayers swing for the fences every time they are at bat in an all-out effort to hit a homerun. Unfortunately for these hitters, they strike out many more times than they round the bases. These "all or nothing" hitters are the equivalent of aggressive investors in the investment world.

Of all the different investment objectives, aggressive growth offers the highest potential for return, along with the highest risk. Investors with this objective seek the greatest reward possible for every dollar invested. Many are drawn to the idea of a get rich quick scheme. Investors with aggressive growth as their goal must be willing to accept the possibility of a loss of a large chunk of their money. The loss of their entire principal is even possible.

You should regard money invested in this style as "play money." You should not have an aggressive growth objective for any money that you need for an important near term expenditure. You should even be wary of investing with an aggressive growth style for important goals that are a far distance in the future.

Just because this strategy carries with it a great deal of risk does not mean you shouldn't apply logic to your investment decisions. Do not speculate in securities or use trading techniques such as shorting and buying on margin without knowing what you are getting into. Taking informed risks is acceptable, taking uninformed risks is not.

Using leverage to supercharge your investment returns is a popular aggressive technique. Not surprisingly, the result is often the loss of the entire small amount of money that is put down. You should research your aggressive investment choices thoroughly and believe that there is a strong chance that the investment will work out. Blindly following a hot tip is bound to lead to disappointment.

People with this aggressive growth objective should be more sophisticated and experienced handling their money than the average investor. Many of the financial instruments employed with this aggressive growth strategy can be complex, and those investing this way should know what they are getting into. There are a few different profiles of individuals who want an aggressive growth objective for part of their portfolio. One prominent group would be individuals who are "risk seekers." Some people psychologically just like taking risks and want their portfolio to be exposed for the chance of a large reward. They want to be where the action is.

Another group of aggressive investors are people who just allot a small portion of their portfolio, for example 5%, to this style, try to hit a homerun with it, and are willing to accept a large loss. The majority of their portfolio is more conservative with a mix of the different asset classes. Lastly, individuals who have a long time frame for a portion of their money that is not crucial to them can afford to be very aggressive. Having a long time horizon gives them more leeway to make up any losses that occur. Because the money was not for something imperative, such investors find it easier to accept the loss if they are not able to make up for it.

The common requirements of all aggressive investors are that they should be keenly aware of the risks and that they be able to stomach the ups and downs that come with this objective. You need the constitution to handle extreme market swings. Do not be one of those people who think they can handle extreme volatility, but who, in reality, cannot. You should remember back to the reaction you had the last time there was a sharp decline in one of your assets. Did you shrug it off or did it bother you for months? Simply put, never put at stake any money that you cannot afford to lose.

For true aggressive growth investors, individual securities or derivatives based on them should be the investment product of choice. Single security risk is desired. The diversification offered by mutual funds and exchange-traded funds works against getting the supersized return an aggressive growth investor craves. Even funds of a single country, a single sector, or ones that call themselves aggressive, by the very nature of their having multiple securities in their offering are not truly aggressive growth. Even when a market is hot, it is rare to see a mutual fund or exchange-traded fund with a yearly return of over 100%. Aggressive growth investors are willing to accept the volatility and risk needed for the potential for huge gains—the fewer the securities, the higher the risk, the higher the return potential. They recognize that they are taking a big chance with the money devoted to this strategy.

Aggressive portfolios commonly use equities and derivatives of equities, including call and put options. The equities chosen are often small caps and micro caps with market capitalizations below $1 billion. These stocks are often the worst of both worlds: they are illiquid, yet highly volatile. Earnings are usually nonexistent and debt levels are generally high. Few, if any, research analysts provide buy, hold, and sell recommendations. Many have prices below $10 and are regularly on the list of the best and worst percentage performers on the three major U.S. exchanges for a given day.

The only time money market and short-term bonds are used in an aggressive strategy is as a holding place for your cash before you decide where to invest it. Fixed income and money market instruments play a minimal role for people with an aggressive growth objective. This crowd frowns upon low return with low risk.

An aggressive growth strategy can include investments in real estate and commodities. Pools of commodity stocks and REITs are not aggressive enough for these investors. However, physical real estate and commodities and futures and options based on real estate and commodities do provide tremendous return potential with a lot of risk. These products offer a lot of opportunities to leverage your original investment and control a large amount of capital with a small amount of money down. The riskiest real estate venture is probably buying raw land and the riskiest commodity is buying commodity futures.

Some aggressive investors like to employ a strategy of constant short-term trading of their account. Despite a lot of hype, very few day traders are successful over time. Although some trades you make may be very profitable, in the end the various costs will bury your performance. Taxes and brokerage fees will take out the biggest bite.

When you constantly buy and sell securities, you need your win rate to be very high. Tremendous outperformance of a security usually occurs over months and years not minutes and seconds. Overall, short term day trading is gambling, not investing. The parties that benefit the most from day traders are their broker and the IRS.

Investing based on momentum is another popular strategy. The philosophy is to buy what is going up and sell what is moving down. The mantra is "the trend is your friend." The fundamentals of the investment are an afterthought. Momentum works when the trend in the market continues, but it gets slammed when the market reverses itself.

The market is more efficient than most people think. When inefficiencies exist, they do not last long. Also, if you factor in your transaction costs, some inefficiencies would not be worth acting on.

If there were a strategy that consistently produced outsized returns, more and more people would use it. As more people employ the strategy, the harder it would be to produce the strong return numbers. With the Internet and widespread business news, strategies that work are harder to keep secret. Furthermore, historically markets have been cyclical. One year one sector is hot; another year another sector is the star performer. Never does one sector of the market go straight up; there are always some down periods.

If you are a very aggressive investor, you can modestly protect yourself. After you buy a security, establish price points where you will automatically sell it. This is especially relevant if the price falls below the purchase price. For example, you can say you will only accept a 25% loss. This will protect you somewhat and not cause a tremendous amount of turnover. By having this automatic selling price, you reduce your downside risk and take some of the emotional elements out of the investment decision.

There are different degrees of aggressive investing. This chapter has discussed *extreme* aggressive investing. I do not recommend putting a large portion of your assets in a single call option, raw undeveloped land, or in a commodity futures contract, even if you are a knowledgeable aggressive investor.

I believe in a moderate aggressive growth objective. This is an approach that is more aggressive than a growth strategy, but not so aggressive that you might lose your entire investment. Mutual funds that focus on riskier parts of the equity market, exchange-traded funds that concentrate on a specific industry sector or emerging market would be the kinds of investments I would prefer for a part of your portfolio if you have an aggressive growth goal. Owning a pool of speculative securities makes me feel more comfortable than having a single risky security or derivative comprising the aggressive growth portion of your portfolio.

The following screens would be examples of the types of aggressive investments I would favor. The chance for outsized returns with exotic instruments and in exotic markets many times comes with high costs attached. It is important to try to keep your costs as low as possible. Your costs are more or less fixed; your future returns are much more unpredictable, especially when you invest with an aggressive growth objective.

Figure 13.1 screens for domestic equity mutual funds that have had annualized returns greater than 25% over the last 1-, 3-, and 5-year periods. Each fund has to have had the same portfolio manager for at least the past 5 years. To be selected the fund has to require $10,000 or less as a minimum initial investment, be a no-load, and have an expense ratio below 1. The screen outputs real estate and commodity sector funds.

An investor with an aggressive growth objective may want to consider the no-load international mutual funds shown in Figure 13.2. Here all the funds selected have had above a 30% annualized return over the last 1-, 3-, and 5-year periods. Each requires $3,000 or less for an initial investment. To keep your costs low, each fund also has an expense ratio below 1.50. International funds are more expensive to run than domestic funds so the expense ratio threshold for these funds is higher than the funds in Figure 13.1. If you buy exchange-traded funds, you need to use a broker, which is an added expense.

Distribution of Asset Classes within an Aggressive Growth Strategy

Aggressive investing leads you to asset classes that offer you the highest return potential. Risk is going to be very prevalent with this strategy. This is the area of your portfolio where chances can be taken. Stocks should be the highest weight asset class in aggressive growth because of their capital appreciation potential. Small cap and international stocks should be a large component of the equity portion. Derivatives to hedge positions in your portfolio can be incorporated into the other investment strategies. However, derivatives whose purpose is to take advantage of leverage for the potential of tremendous returns are appropriate for aggressive investing only. Real estate and commodities also offer high

Figure 13.1 High Risk-High Return Domestic Funds With Low Expenses As of 6/30/07

Search Criteria

U.S. Markets

	Low Value	High Value
Total Return 1 Year	25%	
Total Return 3 Years	25%	
Total Return 5 Years	25%	
Expense Ratio		1.00
Manager Since	2002	
Minimum Investment		$10,000

Output

Symbol	Mutual Fund	Total Return 1 Year	Annualized Total Return 3 Years	Annualized Total Return 5 Years	Expense Ratio	Manager Tenure	Minimum Investment
CGMRX	CGM Realty	35.83%	35.77%	33.11%	0.88	13 Years	$2,500
HGCIX	Hartford Global Comm HLS IA	35.06%	26.40%	25.16%	0.64	7 Years	$0
VGPMX	Vanguard Precious Metals and Mining	28.63%	43.61%	29.13%	0.35	11 Years	$10,000

Figure 13.2 High Risk-High Return International Funds with Low Expenses As of 6/30/07

Search Criteria

International Markets	Low Value	High Value
Total Return 1 Year	30%	
Total Return 3 Years	30%	
Total Return 5 Years	30%	
Expense Ratio		1.50
Manager Since	2002	
Minimum Investment		$3,000

Output

Symbol	Fund	Annualized Total Return 1 Year	Annualized Total Return 3 Years	Total Return 5 Years	Expense Ratio	Minimum Investment
AEMGX	Acadian Emerging Markets	36.32%	42.16%	33.01%	1.38	$2,500
DFCSX	DFA Continental Small Company	42.11%	37.67%	31.54%	0.61	$1
DEMSX	DFA Emerging Markets Small Cap	56.89%	41.18%	32.91%	0.81	$1
DFEVX	DFA Emerging Markets	56.18%	46.49%	36.57%	0.22	$1,000
TREMX	T Rowe Price Emerging Europe & Mediterranean	33.97%	40.81%	35.89%	1.26	$3,000

Figure 13.3 Asset Mix for Aggressive Growth Strategy

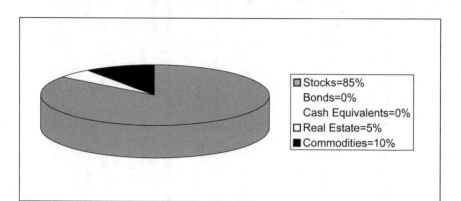

☐ Stocks=85%
  Bonds=0%
  Cash Equivalents=0%
☐ Real Estate=5%
■ Commodities=10%

return potential and have low correlation to the equity market. Fixed income and cash instruments should not be included in an aggressive investment strategy because their return potential is limited. Figure 13.3 illustrates the asset mix typical of an aggressive growth strategy.

Points to Remember

- Aggressive growth offers the highest potential returns, along with the highest risk of all of the different investment objectives.
- You should not have an aggressive growth objective for any money that you need for an important expenditure in the next 12 months.
- All aggressive investors must be able to stomach the ups and downs that come with seeking aggressive growth returns.
- If you are an aggressive growth investor, I suggest you own a pool of speculative securities.
- Constant short term trading is a losing strategy.
- You can protect yourself a little by deciding right after you buy a security at what price you will automatically sell it.

PART IV

SUMMING IT UP

CHAPTER 14

TEN WAYS TO GROW AND ENSURE WEALTH

Investing is simple, but not easy.

WARREN BUFFETT

Any psychologist will tell you that along with death and public speaking, money matters always rank as one of peoples' biggest fears. Many worry about being able to afford to feed and clothe their family and provide them with a safe place to live. We all know that today, these necessities do not come cheap. It doesn't help that many times people waste some of their financial resources. In handling their money, individuals make lots of foolish mistakes. Often errors get compounded into more errors, creating undue hardship.

Unfortunately, there are not many formal avenues to teach people simple financial skills. Trial and error is the method employed by the masses. Currently, basic money management courses are sorely lacking at the high school and college level. The result is that some people are financially illiterate when they enter the workforce. They are often blindly taken advantage of by financial institutions and unscrupulous professionals. Many investors end up letting other people make financial decisions for them. Some of these other people often have less knowledge than the actual investors would have if the investors took the time and had the opportunity to learn about investing.

To create and ensure wealth for yourself and your loved ones, it is important for you to educate yourself and learn as much as you can about money and investing. Try to read at least one investment-related book per year and keep up with the latest financial news through newspapers, magazines, business-related television programs, and websites. Unlike some investing styles, there is no downside to gaining knowledge. Furthermore, curious and inquisitive individuals are usually the most successful investors.

You should focus on the aspects of your financial life that you can control. The percentage you save from your take-home pay, the amount you invest regularly, and the percentages you allocate to different assets are the types of things that you can control. On the other hand, the future returns of an asset are largely out of your control. What follows is a discussion of those aspects of your financial life that you should learn to control to grow and ensure wealth.

1. Own Financial Assets

In most cases, in order to accumulate and ensure wealth, you are going to have to invest in the financial markets. You have to be in the game. You cannot expect to become wealthy just sticking your money in a piggy bank. Your money should work for you, getting positive returns. In order to create wealth from your assets, you have to take some risk. If it were easy and riskless, everybody would be a millionaire.

You need to take some chances with your portfolio. It is better to take chances in the asset class you understand best and that is somewhat volatile. You are not going to make a killing investing in safe instruments such as certificates of deposit or savings bonds, no matter what your expertise is with these instruments. You have to invest in an asset class that offers the possibility of higher returns. Ask yourself, does an investment in this asset have a good chance of doubling in five years? Use whatever strengths and special know-how you have when you invest. For example, if you know a lot about the biotech industry, when you feel the time is right and some of the stocks are at an attractive price, you should buy a few of the stocks you think can sharply appreciate. Of course, don't ignore your overall asset allocation in determining how much to invest in biotech stocks. You should still have exposure to other equities, bonds, and money market instruments.

2. Start Investing When You Are Young

The saying "good habits start young" definitely applies to managing your money. Investing at an early age is a point I have reiterated.

Your money has a longer time to compound the sooner it is invested. Over time, the earnings, dividends, and coupons you receive when they are reinvested back into your portfolio can amount to serious money. Money compounded over 30 years accumulates much more than money compounded for 15 years.

By starting young, you are also getting a head start on your savings. The chances you can take and the investing options available to you are generally higher the earlier you start putting money in the financial markets. Furthermore, by starting at an early age you will be learning about investing. Textbook learning is helpful in investing, but it is no substitute for the knowledge learned from actually doing it. Experience is the best teacher. While you are young, there is time to make up for any mistakes you make and the opportunity to learn from your financial mishaps and correct them in the future.

3. Invest Regularly

Regardless of the amounts, it is important to invest in regular intervals. This allows you to avoid investing a big lump sum at the top of the market and not investing at all at the bottom. Nobody has the ability to perfectly time markets. Investors who try to time the market are essentially saying that they can buy an investment when it's at its lowest point and sell it at its highest. Furthermore, by trying to time the market, there is often a "cash drag" which occurs if you are sitting on the sidelines in cash instruments when other asset classes are performing well. Dollar cost averaging, a simple investing technique where you invest the same amount every period, is widely encouraged by investment professionals. Diversifying when you invest, along with what you invest in, is an easy and effective way to reduce your risk.

By allotting a percentage of your income to your 401(k) plan each paycheck, you can be investing automatically. You do not have to write a check every time you want to contribute. In addition, you never have physical possession of this chunk of your money, so you are not tempted to spend it on discretionary items. If you have to stop and write a check for your retirement contribution, you may avoid doing it. Or there may be some near-term financial worry that may divert your funds. For those without access to 401(k) plans, there are automatic asset builder programs available. These accounts take money from your paycheck or bank account—often as little as $50 per month—and invest it automatically according to your direction. Major mutual fund firms such as Fidelity and Vanguard offer automatic asset builder programs.

4. Diversify Your Assets

It is important to spread your risk around. All your assets should not be in one single security or even one asset class. You do not want the sharp percentage decline in one of your assets to mean an equal percentage decline in your net worth. There is no way to avoid risk completely if you are investing in the financial markets. Diversification does not ensure a profit. It though is an easy way to alleviate some downside risk.

You can achieve this goal by buying different asset classes and some different segments within those asset classes. Your portfolio needs to consist of some investments that have very low correlations to one another. You want some holdings zigging when others are zagging. By doing this, losses in some assets can be made up with gains from others. A key to effective diversification is to make sure that each investment fulfills a separate and distinct purpose for your overall financial strategy. If you cannot explain in a few simple sentences why something is in your portfolio, it probably should not be in there.

Lack of financial resources is not a valid excuse for not being diversified. Balanced mutual funds provide a way to get a mix of asset classes in a single investment at a reasonable cost. Many require only $2,500 to open up and have expense ratios below 1%.

5. Limit Your Use of Credit

There is a simple equation in finance: assets minus liabilities equal net worth. Most people spend their time and energy focusing on increasing their assets to increase their wealth. In many cases, controlling your liabilities is an easier solution.

Overextending yourself by taking on too much debt is a potential killer for your financial well-being. It is better to avoid the problem by limiting your use of credit, especially high interest credit. Compounding works very much in your favor when it works its magic on your assets. It works to your detriment when it comes to your debt.

You do need some credit. Most people need loans to help pay for a house, car, and tuition. Even when borrowing for these important purchases try not to overextend yourself. Try to keep the balance manageable and shop around to get the best interest rate possible. If you threaten to switch to another credit card provider, your current provider often gives you better terms on your existing card to keep your business. Overall, paying off debt as quickly as possible should be a priority in your plans, not a luxury.

Credit for essential items in your life can be classified as good credit; credit used on nonessential items is bad credit. The average American household with at least one credit card has nearly $9,200 in credit card debt according to CardWeb.com. Avoid overpurchasing on your credit cards like the plague. Credit card debt is the most expensive debt. Some call it the *anti-investment*. Credit cards come with interest rates that make your balances compound exponentially when they are not paid off on time.

There is no investment that can consistently outperform the interest rate charged on outstanding credit card debt. Do not purchase items on your credit cards that you cannot pay off immediately when the bill comes in the mail, especially items that are consumed quickly like meals or a vacation. If you just pay the minimum balance, your debt will keep growing and growing. Furthermore, your credit score will take a severe hit, making it more expensive and difficult to borrow for future purchases. Carrying credit card debt repeatedly is a sign that you are living beyond your means.

If you have gotten into trouble using credit cards in the past, try using cash for your purchases. Studies have found that people who use cash instead of credit cards spend less. Even though both are real money, the fact that you actually see physical cash leaving your wallet and going to a cashier makes it seem more tangible and more difficult to part with.

6. Be Conscious of Costs

You should aim to have the maximum amount of your investable dollars working for you. Hard work went into accumulating your assets; your money should work hard as well. Fees, commissions, and taxes cut into every investor's pocket. No doubt about it, by putting money into the financial markets, you will incur costs. There is, however, a wide range of costs for similar products and services.

You should not blindly give your money to a financial firm. You need to comparison shop when looking for a broker, mutual fund, or exchange-traded fund. Know how the financial firm is being compensated and what you are getting for your money. At a minimum, know how much it costs to buy, manage, and sell the investment. Keep in mind that financial firms are in business to make a profit. You need to avoid high commissions on stock trades, loads on mutual funds, and high expense ratios on mutual and exchange-traded funds. Reasononably priced brokerage and money management services are widely available. Many provide equal or better results than their higher-cost brethren.

7. Live Below Your Means

No matter how much money is coming into your household, you should make a conscious effort to see that your expenses are less. It is important to try to make this spread between your income and your expenses as large as possible. Try to target saving at least 10% of your income. People with high incomes sometimes go into bankruptcy because their spending gets out of control. Ultimately, how you handle money is more important than how much you earn.

Without net savings you will not have capital to invest. To grow your wealth you need a source of funds to invest. Clearly, everyone has some required expenses. I am not advocating sleeping on the street or going on a hunger strike to lower your bills. You though should be aware of your expenses and try to reduce them where it is prudent. In many cases tough choices and sacrifices are going to have to be made. Items such as not getting the premium cable package, reducing the number of minutes on your cell phone plan, and bringing your lunch to work can take a bite out of your monthly bills over time. Saving a few dollars each day compounds into quite a bit of money over time. David Bach wrote a bestselling book, *The Automatic Investor*, which stressed this very point.

You should know what percentage you are spending on needs (housing, food, transportation, clothes) and how much you are spending on discretionary items. The necessities should be satisfied before the wants are addressed in your budget. Within the needs, there is a wide range you can spend. There is a big difference between the cost of a Ferrari and a Toyota Corolla and a big difference between clothes bought at Barneys and those bought at Old Navy. Individuals should try to target their "essential" expenses to be no more than 50% of their after-tax income.

Avoid comparing yourself financially to others. Trying to keep up with the Joneses is stupid; rather, budget your money so you can sleep at night. The person down the block with the McMansion and the Mercedes and the Lexus in the driveway may be carrying massive amounts of debt. They may be living paycheck to paycheck and sweating when their monthly mortgage and car bills come every month. Do not be fooled; appearances can be deceiving when it comes to money. Spending money and actually having the money to spend can be two totally different things.

8. Spend on What Is Really Important

Everyone has different wants and desires. After your basic needs are covered, you should spend your discretionary money on things that are of high importance to you. For one person it might mean buying a Harley-Davidson motorcycle, for another it might mean paying for their child's tuition. You should do a self-evaluation to determine what is most important to you.

You do not want the majority of your discretionary income going to things that have little meaning to you. Track your expenses for a couple of months to see where your money is actually going. Many times people are shocked when they see how much they spend on meaningless items. Spending money on the things that are important to you is bound to make you feel good and help your psyche.

Adequate insurance should be high on the list of spending priorities. Protecting your assets is as important as trying to obtain them. You do not want to make a tragedy even worse by not getting some kind of monetary compensation for your dependents.

9. Allot Time to Doing Something You Love

In today's fast-paced world, nobody has the time to do everything they want in a given day. We have many constraints: work, commuting, and family to name just a few. Despite our busy lives, it is important in this framework to allot some time to something that you love doing. Some people find it in their job or hobby; others may find it in reading a story to their young daughter before she goes to bed.

It gives us motivation and a reason to get up in the morning when we know that we will spend at least a little bit of time doing something that makes us very happy. Furthermore, the essential activities of our life that we do not care for become a little more bearable when we know that we will be doing something we thoroughly enjoy in the very near future. True wealth is not only in your wallet but also in your heart.

10. Trust Your Inner Voice When You Invest

There is a funny episode of *Seinfeld* where the character George Costanza does the opposite of every instinct. George has had no success in his life doing the things that he thought were right at the time, so he then decides to try the opposite approach. In the episode, this approach works for a while and then does George in at the end. In your investing life, you should dismiss George's scheme.

I believe that people should trust their inner voice when investing. Follow your instincts. If an investment makes you uncomfortable for whatever reason, you should avoid it. There are plenty of alternatives you can choose from. Be as knowledgeable as possible regarding investment choices. Try to keep up with the financial news of the day. In other words, stay tuned in. Read and learn as much as you can about the investments you are considering buying. When you go to sleep at night you should have a clear and worry-free conscious about how you chose your investments.

Points to Remember

If you abide by the following recommendations, you will substantially increase your chances of becoming wealthy:

- Have exposure to financial assets.
- Start investing when you are young.
- Invest regularly.

- Diversify your investments.
- Limit your use of debt.
- Be conscious of costs and try to minimize them.
- Live below your means.
- Spend on what is really important to you.
- Allot time to doing something you love.
- Trust your inner voice when you invest.

CHAPTER 15

PUTTING IT ALL TOGETHER

The distance is nothing; it is only the first step that is difficult.

MARIE ANNE DU DEFFAND

Managing your personal portfolio can seem very complicated. There appear to be so many moving parts—stocks, bonds, mutual funds, exchange-traded funds, interest rate hikes, taxes, housing crashes, recessions, bull markets, bear markets. You should not be overwhelmed. If you take a step back and try to understand what your goals are for your assets, the picture can become much clearer. Block out the day-to-day noise and focus on the longer-term picture. Investing is a marathon, not a sprint. Slow and steady usually wins the race.

Here's one convenient way to put together the many ideas of this book and make the most of your financial resources. Look at your personal money management and asset allocation decisions through the prism of five basic questions:

- Who?
- Why?
- When?
- Where?
- How? (The most debated question.)

Focus on your asset allocation because it is the major driver in the success or failure of your investment plan. Security selection may be the sexier subject but the percentages you choose for the different asset classes will be the bigger determinant of your overall investment returns.

Who?

It is important for you or anyone else who has money in financial assets to know themselves. You need to have a good feel for the amount of risk you are willing to take. Are you superaggressive, very conservative, or like the vast majority somewhere in between? You need to know what the goals are for your money and how many actual dollars you need to achieve those goals. Most people have multiple goals. It is imperative that your money is segregated so that certain accounts can be targeted for specific goals. For example, your retirement account should be separate from your checking account. Overall, there will probably be some accounts in which you can take some chances and others in which you do not want a modicum of risk. Your willingness to take risks will probably change over time given changes in your circumstances.

You also need to determine if you require outside help with your investments. Some investors may want to hire an advisor because of their own perceived lack of knowledge. Others may want to hire an advisor because they do not want to take the required time and effort in determining which asset classes they should have and which securities in them to buy and sell. It is not a sign of weakness that you want assistance. When deciding to get help do your due diligence to make sure that the advisor that you are hiring is competent and trustworthy and the services offered are worth the cost. A goal of all investors should be to eventually learn enough so that they can minimize their use of an advisor. Remember, a financial professional can never have as much interest in your well-being as you, yourself, have.

Be skeptical of any get-rich-quick schemes. Delete the e-mail that tells you that XYZ stock trading at 20 cents a share is due to go up tenfold in the next month because the company has a breakthrough drug that is the cure for cancer. Do not watch the infomercial telling you that you can make millions in real estate without putting any money down for the properties. Throw away the fax that states that ABC stock is going to go up substantially because the company has come up with a process of turning water into oil. Scrutinize the source of your investment advice. Caveat emptor—anything that sounds too good to be true probably is a scam.

Why?

There is definitely more to life than money. Money, though, makes a lot of things in life easier. Life's necessities of food, shelter, and clothing require significant capital. Very few of us hunt for our own food, build our own home, and make our own clothes.

By managing your money wisely, more of your investment goals can be fulfilled. Bad money management can thwart the achievement of your goals and can create financial havoc for some. Whether your goal is retiring at an earlier age, sending your child to an Ivy League school without massive student loans, or going on a cruise around the world, more money opens up the door to more options and possibilities than less money. More choices are better than fewer choices. Do not let money be the gatekeeper that prevents you from getting things that are very important to you. Trying to make life a little better for yourself and your loved ones should serve as the only motivation you need to do the best job you can managing your money.

When?

When should you start to invest in the financial markets? My response is right now. If this isn't possible, you should save and invest as soon as you can. Do not play games and try to perfectly time the market, since it is a skill no one has. Nobody knows when we are at the exact top or exact bottom of the market. You are better off investing consistently in regular amounts over time.

Prognosticating is a major mistake. Time is one of your biggest allies in growing your portfolio. By not putting money in the markets, you are giving up the chance of compounding your assets. Every day your money is sitting idle it is giving up the chance to earn capital gains and income. The more time your money has in which to work, the more it can earn. Furthermore, it is easier to ride out periods of bad returns when you start earlier. No one ever became rich by keeping their money on the sidelines forever.

You should address goals such as financing your child's college education and providing for your retirement when your child is born and when you start working. Do not delay. Accounts should be opened up early, not close to the target date when the money is going to be needed. Generally, the earlier you start investing for a goal, the better the chance you will reach the goal.

Where?

Your money should be invested in multiple asset classes. Stocks, bonds, cash instruments, real estate, and commodities should be represented in everyone's portfolio. How much of these assets you own will depend on your personal circumstances. Within these asset classes, there are numerous choices available. In varying degrees, everyone should have assets that provide growth potential and those that provide safe, steady returns.

Look at past returns for assets, but do not take them as a given for what the future will hold for them. As the ubiquitous financial disclaimer states: "Past returns are no guarantee of future performance." It is wise to have a forecast for what you are expecting for your securities in the future. An entry point and exit price where you would buy and sell an asset is advised. Taking some of the emotion out of an investment decision is generally helpful for your investment results.

Before placing money in the markets, you should perform a personal financial checkup. You need to know where you stand before you start investing. If you do not know where you are now, how are you going to get where you want to be? You need to figure out how much insurance you need, how large an emergency fund to set aside, and the value of your major assets and liabilities.

Most people know in exact detail what their income is. They should be equally aware of how and where their money is being spent. Many times there is a high percentage of their money going to unnecessary discretionary items.

While the investments you have should be diverse, you should limit the number of financial services firms you use. You do not want all your assets to be with one firm. By the same token, you do not want your assets with so many firms that they are hard to keep track of and get you bogged down in paperwork. Two money management firms and two banks are more than enough as repositories for your money. Keep it simple. It is much easier for you to stay organized if you have your money deposited in just a few financial firms. It helps you keep track of your investments and makes it easier to spot if you need some adjustments to your portfolio. Ultimately, better organization gives you a better chance of reaching your goals.

How?

To decide how to invest your money, you should have a specific goal and dollar amount you are trying to accumulate. The odds of hitting your target increase exponentially when you aim at it. Separate accounts should have specific objectives. Commingling your accounts will likely cause some goals not to be fulfilled. Your asset allocation should incorporate your risk tolerance and when your money will be needed.

Every portfolio should have some exposure to the major asset classes of equities, fixed income, and money market instruments. There should also be some funds set aside for a real estate and commodity position. Your risk should be spread around. Your overall portfolio should not be highly concentrated (more than 75%) in an asset class and especially it should not have an extremely high percentage in an individual security (no more than 10%). One security's return should not dominate an entire portfolio's performance.

The bulk of your investments should be in low-cost mutual funds and ETFs. These investments provide diversification, liquidity, low minimums, convenience and, in the case of actively managed mutual funds, professional portfolio management. Do not chase hot funds which recently had strong performance. Rather, choose low-cost funds with good long term track records whose current portfolio manager delivered the performance.

Asset allocation and life cycle funds are a particularly good place in which to have a large percentage of your money. These funds can specifically target the investment objectives of your time horizon or your risk tolerance with a diversified portfolio. Besides having numerous holdings, these types of funds are diversified at the asset class level. After you have a diversified base for your portfolio, you can add specialized individual securities as you see fit.

Everyone hopes for the best returns they can possibly get on their assets. Future returns, though, are unpredictable. The fees and expenses you pay on your investments, however, are much easier to determine. Keeping your costs under control can save thousands of dollars over the course of a lifetime. The difference between owning mutual funds with loads and expense ratios over 1.5% and owning no-load mutual funds with expense ratios of 0.50% is huge. Do not give away money to high-cost financial firms when there are cheaper products of the same quality available elsewhere. Your money should work for you, not for your broker's bank account.

Take advantage of tax deferred accounts such as retirement and educational accounts. Try to put your more tax-efficient investments such as index mutual funds and exchange-traded funds in your taxable accounts and your less tax efficient ones, including actively managed mutual funds and corporate bonds, in your nontaxable accounts. Tax implications should not dominate your investment decisions, but all things being equal, they can be the tipping point. Do not give money to the IRS if you do not have to.

It bears repeating that it is important to start investing as early as possible. The earlier you start, the more the magic of compounding can do for your portfolio and the easier it is to ride out the inevitable periods of down markets. Breaking your portfolio into several asset classes and several assets within each asset class will also reduce your risk. Giving up some upside returns is more than worth the huge downside risk that is reduced by diversification. For the equity portion of your portfolio, I would advise that if you cannot afford to own at least 20 stocks in different industries, you should anchor this part of your assets with a diversified low-cost index mutual fund or exchange-traded fund.

You should know why each asset is in your portfolio. If you cannot easily explain why a security is in your portfolio, you should not own it. Safety, diversification, income generation, and capital appreciation potential are all worthwhile reasons for you to own a security. Never invest in any asset that makes you feel uncomfortable.

There are plenty of choices available in the financial world. More and more investment products are being created every day. Find and put money in those that you understand and that allow you to sleep at night.

After securities are chosen, your job is not done. You need to monitor how the security is performing compared to a relevant benchmark and whether there is any significant news that may change the investment outlook. Buy and forget is a recipe for failure. At a minimum, you should review the assets in your portfolio two times during the year. Consider rebalancing if an asset class has moved more than 5% away from its desired weight. Do not rebalance just to rebalance. Have a sound reason why you are adjusting your portfolio.

In the end, your asset allocation is a very personal choice. I have provided you with the tools to build a low-cost diversified portfolio and suggested what your rational expectations should be. Furthermore, I have cautioned you to be prepared and not be blindsided by unforeseen events which could cause your portfolio to suffer massive losses. A well-crafted plan of action can help you weather all sorts of changing market conditions as you aim to meet your investment goals. Ultimately, successful investment planning is about finding the mix of assets that lets you aim for the return you want, with a level of risk you can handle.

Benjamin Franklin once said: "An investment in knowledge always pays the best interest." I hope that you learned a lot from this book and that you will be more comfortable putting together your investment portfolio. I am confident that if you take the advice offered here, your overall financial health will improve.

INDEX

Aggressive growth
  approach for, 191–192
  asset allocation with, 192
  asset classes distribution with,
    195, 198
  with bonds, 193
  day trading for, 193
  with equities, 193
  with individual securities, 192–193
  momentum investing for, 194
  protection for, 194
  with real estate, 193
  risk v. return of, 191–192
  screens of mutual funds for, 195–197
Aggressive growth funds, 59–60
Alternative minimum tax (AMT), 39
AMT. See Alternative minimum tax
Annual percentage yield (APY), 151
Annuities
  bonds v., 167
  conservative income with, 166–167
  fees of, 167
  fixed v. variable, 167
APY. See Annual percentage yield
Asset allocation. See also Strategic
    asset allocation; Tactical asset
    allocation

age v. stage of life when considering,
    4–5, 116
with aggressive growth, 192
asset classes and, 16–17, 19
of bonds, 10–11, 17
buy and hold strategy for, 12
common example of, 25–26
considerations for, 115, 135–136
daily examples of, 13
early career and, 116–121
economic scenarios impacting,
    105–106
financial status determining, 142
goals for, 143
hedge funds and, 45
insured asset allocation strategy
    for, 12
investment products for, 22–23
late career considerations for,
    123–124
long term goals v. short term
    goals for, 127
male v. female considerations for, 138
married v. single concerns for, 139
middle career considerations for,
    121–122
of mutual funds, 21, 26

Asset allocation (*Continued*)
  organization of, 24–25, 214–215
  personal knowledge and, 202
  portfolio and, 1–6, 10, 17–19, 67,
    110–111, 211, 214–217
  procedure for, 13
  process of, 10, 26–27
  questions regarding, 9–10
  reassessing, 23–24
  REITs and, 18
  retirement considerations for,
    124–126
  risk tolerance and, 128–133
  risk *v.* return in, 2, 10–11
  of securities, 22
  of stocks, 4, 10–11, 17, 34
Asset classes
  aggressive growth distribution of,
    195, 198
  allocation justifications of, 17–18
  asset allocation and, 16–17, 19
  bonds and, 29
  capital preservation and, 149–150,
    154
  cash and, 29
  changes in correlations of, 20
  conservative income distribution
    of, 167–168
  diversification *v.* single security
    risk in, 20, 27
  growth and income distribution
    of, 176–178
  growth distribution of, 189
  inflation and, 179
  product diversity in, 17
  stocks and, 29

Balanced mutual funds
  life cycle funds and, 63
  risk *v.* reward of, 63–64
Bank investment contract (BIC).
    See GICs

Bond mutual funds
  diversification through, 165
  risk *v.* reward of, 61–62
Bonds. *See also* Convertible bonds;
    Corporate bonds; Government
    agency bonds; International
    bonds; Mortgage bonds; Munici-
    pal bonds; Treasury inflation pro-
    tected bonds; Zero coupon bonds
  aggressive growth with, 193
  annuities *v.*, 167
  asset allocation of, 10–11, 17
  asset classes and, 29
  capital preservation with, 150, 155
  cash and stocks *v.*, 30
  conservative income with, 164–165
  credit ratings for measuring, 164
  diversification of, 21
  face value *v.* trading value of, 36–37
  growth and, 188
  growth and income with, 174–176
  individual securities and, 51–52
  interest rates and, 107
  maturity of, 39–40
  portfolio and, 36
  predicting, 37
  risk *v.* stability of, 36–37
  S&P *v.* Moody rating, 38
  stocks *v.*, 36–37, 164–165
  taxes and, 164–165
  Treasury issued *v.* corporate
    issued, 165
Brokers. *See also* Financial advisors
  bid/ask spread and, 93
  discount *v.* full-service, 92–94
  DRIPs *v.*, 94
  experienced investors *v.* novice
    investors and, 140–141
  fees of, 91–94
  limit orders *v.* market orders of,
    92–93
  Treasuries *v.*, 94–95

Buy and hold
    advantages *v.* disadvantages, 14
    asset allocation strategy of, 12

Capital preservation
    asset classes and, 149–150, 154
    with bonds, 150, 155
    CDs and, 149
    with checking and savings
        accounts, 152
    conservative income *v.*, 157
    diversification and, 148
    equities and, 149, 153
    with ETFs, 152–154
    with GICs, 151–152
    laddering for, 149–150, 154
    liquidity and, 147
    with money market accounts, 151
    with money market mutual funds,
        150–151, 154
    with mutual funds, 152–153
    portfolio objectives and, 154–155
    retirement concerns with, 148–149
    risk *v.* reward of, 147–148
    Treasuries and, 149–150
Cash
    asset classes and, 29
    benefits of, 42
    credit spending *v.* spending with, 205
    interest rate resources for, 43–44
    stocks and bonds *v.*, 30
Cash equivalents, 17
    conservative income with, 165–166
    diversification of, 21
    liquidity *v.* yield of, 166
CD. *See* Certificate of deposit
Certificate of deposit (CD)
    capital preservation and, 149
    conservative income with, 166
    money market mutual funds *v.*,
        43–44
Collectibles, 49

Commodities
    diversified indexes of, 47–48
    growth with, 188
    investing in, 47–49
    taxes and, 48
Common stock, 31–33
Conservative income
    with annuities, 166–167
    asset classes distribution within,
        167–168
    with bonds, 164–165
    capital preservation *v.*, 157
    with cash equivalents, 165–166
    with CDs, 166
    dividend safety determination for,
        159–160
    portfolio with, 157–158
    risk *v.* reward of, 158
    with stocks, 158–163
    taxes and, 158
Convertible bonds, 41
    growth and income with,
        175–176
    mutual funds with, 176
Corporate bonds
    advantages of, 175
    government agency bonds *v.*, 37
    municipal bonds *v.*, 38
    risk *v.* reward of, 37–38
    taxes and, 38
Coverdell Education Savings
        Accounts (Coverdell ESAs)
    advantages *v.* disadvantages of, 87
    529 plans *v.*, 87
    taxes and, 87
Credit
    bonds ratings through, 164
    cash spending *v.* spending, 205
    compounding *v.* debt in, 205
    early career danger with,
        120–121
    limiting, 204–205

Derivatives, 52–53, 67
Discount cash flow model, stock
  analysis of, 33–34
Diversification
  of asset classes *v.* single security
    risk, 20, 27
  through bond mutual funds, 165
  of bonds, 21
  capital preservation and, 148
  of cash equivalents, 21
  of equities, 20–21
  with mutual funds, 56
  of portfolio, 19–22, 203–204,
    216–217
  portfolio risks with, 21
Dividend reinvestment plans
  (DRIPs), 94
Dividends
  conservative income and safety
    determination of, 159–160
  corporate considerations for, 160
  ETFs and, 162–163
  growth and, 180
  taxation on, 159
Dollar cost averaging, 22, 203
Dow Jones–AIG Commodities
  Index (DJ-AIGCI), 47–48
DRIPs. *See* Dividend reinvestment
  plans

Early career
  asset allocation and, 116–121
  compounding money in, 117–118,
    202–203, 213
  credit card danger during, 120–
    121
  emergency fund for, 119
  employer-sponsored retirement
    plans during, 119
  equities and, 136
  housing payments during, 117, 119

  investing *v.* spending during, 117,
    202–203
  portfolio considerations during,
    121, 136–137
  retirement accounts during,
    119–120
  retirement *v.*, 5, 136–137
  Roth IRA considerations during,
    119–120
Education. *See also* Coverdell ESAs;
    529 plans
  costs of, 83–84
  for finances, 201–202
  investment accounts for, 83–85
  middle career and accounts for, 122
  retirement accounts *v.* investment
    accounts for, 88
  student loans and, 84
Employer-sponsored retirement
  plans
  benefits of, 74–75, 203
  company stock involvement in,
    75–76
  disadvantages of, 75
  early career and, 119
  IRAs and, 75
  taxes and, 74, 101–102
Equities. *See also* Stocks
  aggressive growth with, 193
  capital preservation and, 149, 153
  diversification of, 20–21
  early career and, 136
  Fair Value ranking for, 161–162
  growth with, 180–188
  inflation and, 108–109
  portfolio and, 29
  STARS for measuring, 161–162
  types of, 35
Equity income funds, 60
Equity mutual funds, 58–59. *See also*
    Aggressive growth funds; Equity

income funds; Growth and
income funds; Growth funds;
International/global funds;
Specialty/sector funds
ETFs. *See* Exchange-traded funds
Exchange-traded funds (ETFs), 48
  benefits of, 67
  capital preservation with, 152–154
  dividends and, 162–163
  foreign high yielding, 163–164
  illegalities and, 66
  individual securities *v.*, 65
  mutual funds *v.*, 65–66
  popularity growth of, 64–65

Fair Value ranking, 161–162
Fees
  of annuities, 167
  avoiding, 205–206, 215–216
  of brokers, 91–94
  of hedge funds, 97–98
  of mutual funds, 95–97
Financial advisors
  background checks for, 140
  determining need for, 212
  experienced investors *v.* novice
    investors and, 140–141
Financial goals
  investment policy statement and, 15
  separating investment accounts
    based on, 15–16, 127, 212, 215
529 plans
  advantages *v.* disadvantages of,
    86–87
  college savings plan of, 86
  Coverdell ESAs *v.*, 87
  prepaid tuition plan of, 85–86
  state to state differences of, 85
  taxes and, 86–87, 101–102
Fixed income security, 36
Foreign stocks, 61

growth with, 187–188
portfolio and, 187–188
risk *v.* reward of, 32–33
401k plan. *See* Employer-sponsored
  retirement plans
Futures
  contract, 54
  spot *v.*, 47

GARP. *See* Growth at a reasonable
  price
GICs. *See* Guaranteed investment
  contracts
Goldman Sachs Commodities
  Index (GSCI), 47–48
Government agency bonds, 37
Growth
  asset classes distribution with, 189
  bonds and, 188
  with commodities, 188
  dividends and, 180
  with equities, 180–188
  with foreign stocks, 187–188
  funds, 60
  GARP *v.*, 183
  growth and income *v.*, 180
  money market accounts and, 188
  with real estate, 188–189
  researching for, 186–187
  screens of stocks for, 181–182
  strategies for, 179–180
  value *v.*, 181
Growth and income
  asset classes distribution with,
    176–178
  with bonds, 174–176
  with convertible bonds, 175–176
  funds, 60
  growth *v.*, 180
  with money market accounts,
    174–176

Growth and income (*Continued*)
  with mutual funds, 176–177
  with real estate, 172
  risk *v.* reward of, 171–172
  with securities, 171–172
  with stocks, 173–174
  strategy of, 171
Growth at a reasonable price (GARP)
  growth and value *v.*, 183
  PEG measurements of, 183, 185
  screens of stocks for, 183, 185
Growth funds, 60
Guaranteed investment contracts
    (GICs), 151–152

Hedge funds
  asset allocation and, 45
  fees associated with, 97–98
  mutual funds *v.*, 98
  risk *v.* reward of, 45

Individual retirement account (IRA)
  deadlines and funding of, 82
  employer-sponsored retirement
    plans and, 75
  Keogh plan *v.*, 76
  Roth IRA *v.*, 78–83
  rules of, 77–78
  taxes and, 77–83, 101–102
Individual securities
  aggressive growth with, 192–193
  bonds and, 51–52
  ETFs *v.*, 65
  risk *v.* reward of, 51–52, 67
  stocks and, 51–52
Inflation. *See also* TIPS
  asset classes and, 179
  equities and, 108–109
  high, 108–109
  low, 109
  risk, 128

stocks *v.*, 31
  Treasuries and, 109
Insured asset allocation
  advantages *v.* disadvantages, 14
  asset allocation strategy of, 12
Interest rates
  bonds and, 107
  falling, 107–108
  high, 106
  low, 106
  portfolio impacted from, 106–108
  resources for cash from, 43–44
  rising, 107
International bonds, 41–42
International/global funds, 61
Investment accounts. *See also* Educa-
    tion; Retirement accounts; Taxable
    accounts; Tax-advantaged accounts
  dangers with separating, 16
  for education, 83–85
  instincts and, 208
  retirement *v.* education, 88
  separating, based on financial
    goals, 15–16, 127, 212, 215
  taxes and, 69–70, 98–99
Investment Company Act, 57
Investment policy statement
  considerations of, 15
  financial goals and, 15
Investment products
  asset allocation and, 22–23
  choosing, 22–23
IRA. *See* Individual retirement
    account

Keogh plan
  IRA *v.*, 76
  rules of, 76–77

Large cap stocks
  categorization of, 32

small cap stocks and mid cap
    stocks *v.*, 31–32
Late career
    asset allocation during, 123–124
    portfolio considerations
        during, 123
    retirement accounts and, 123
    taxes to consider during, 123–124
Liquidation, 33

Mid cap stocks
    categorization of, 32
    small cap stocks and large cap
        stocks *v.*, 31–32
Middle career
    asset allocation during, 121–122
    education accounts during, 122
    insurance concerns during, 122
    parenting costs during, 121
    retirement accounts and, 122
    taxes during, 122
Money market accounts
    APY comparisons for, 151
    capital preservation with, 151
    growth and, 188
    growth and income with, 174–176
Money market mutual funds, 42–43
    capital preservation with,
        150–151, 154
    CDs *v.*, 43–44
    risk *v.* reward of, 62–63
Morgan Stanley Capital Interna-
    tional indexes (MSCI indexes),
    S&P 500 *v.*, 33
Morningstar's Portfolio X-Ray, 21
Mortgage bonds, 41
Municipal bonds
    AMT and, 39
    corporate bonds *v.*, 38
    risk *v.* reward of, 38–39
    taxable accounts and, 71–72

taxes and, 38–39, 101
    types of, 39
Mutual funds, 54–55. *See also*
    Balanced mutual funds; Bond
    mutual funds; Equity mutual
    funds; Money market mutual
    funds
    asset allocation and, 21, 26
    benefits of, 55–56
    capital preservation with,
        152–153
    choosing, 64, 67
    convertible bonds in, 176
    diversification with, 56
    ETFs *v.*, 65–66
    expense ratio of, 96
    fees associated with, 95–97
    growth and income with, 176–177
    hedge funds *v.*, 98
    illegalities associated with,
        57–58
    load, 95–97
    NAV and, 56–57
    no-load, 97
    open-end funds *v.* closed-end
        funds in, 55
    popularity growth of, 55
    regulation of, 56–58
    screens for, 162–163
    screens for aggressive growth,
        195–197
    shares classes of, 95
    taxes and, 100–101

Net asset value (NAV), 56–57

Options
    call *v.* put, 53
    components of, 53
    covered call writing with, 54
    uses of, 53–54

PEG. *See* Price/earnings ratio to growth rate

Portfolio
asset allocation and, 1–6, 10, 17–19, 67, 110–111, 211, 214–217
bonds and, 36
capital preservation objectives for, 154–155
catastrophe impacting, 110–111
common asset allocation within, 25–26
conservative income objective for, 157–158
dependents *v.* no dependents and, 141
diversification of, 19–22, 203–204, 216–217
early career considerations for, 121, 136–137
efficiency of, 16–17
equities and, 29
falling interest rates impacting, 107–108
financial risk within, 18–19
financial status and managing, 142
financial windfall impacting, 111
foreign stocks and, 187–188
goals for, 143–144, 213–214
growing economy impacting, 109–110
high inflation impacting, 108–109
high interest rates impacting, 106
late career considerations for, 123
low inflation impacting, 109
low interest rates impacting, 106
male *v.* female considerations for, 138
married *v.* single concerns for, 139
monitoring, 23, 216–217
rebalancing of, 24, 217
recession impacting, 110
retirement and growth of, 126

rising interest rates impacting, 107
risk tolerance with, 5, 202
Preferred stock, 33
Price/earnings ratio to growth rate (PEG), 183, 185

Real estate
aggressive growth with, 193
growth and income with, 172
growth with, 188–189
investing in, 45–47
REITs *v.*, 46
Real estate investment trusts (REITs)
asset allocation and, 18
real estate *v.*, 46
risk *v.* reward of, 46–47
taxes and, 46, 72–73
Rebalancing, of portfolio, 24
REITs. *See* Real estate investment trusts
Relative valuation, of stock, 34
Retirement
asset allocation during, 124–126
capital preservation concerns with, 148–149
early career *v.*, 5, 136–137
expenses *v.* income during, 125–126
Medicare and Social Security considerations in, 3, 124–126
portfolio growth during, 126
will creation during, 137
Retirement accounts. *See also* Employer-sponsored retirement plans; Keogh plan; Roth IRA
early career and, 119–120
education accounts *v.*, 88
health considerations with, 73
late career and, 123
middle career and, 122
restrictions determining, 83

retirement income *v.*, 73–74,
  125–126
Risk
  diversification and, 21
  financial, of portfolio, 18–19
  single security, 20, 27
  of stocks, 4, 30–31
Risk tolerance
  asset allocation and, 128–133
  inflation risk and, 128
  market risk and, 128
  outlier concerns for, 132–133
  portfolio considerations with, 5, 202
  questionnaires for, 129–132
  standard deviation measurements
    for, 128
  tracking error measurements for,
    128, 132
  VaR measurements for, 132
Risk *v.* return
  of aggressive growth, 191–192
  in asset allocation, 2, 10–11
Risk *v.* reward
  of annuities, 166
  of balanced mutual funds, 63–64
  of bond mutual funds, 61–62
  of bonds, 36–37
  of capital preservation, 147–148
  of conservative income, 158
  of corporate bonds, 37–38
  of derivatives, 52–53, 67
  of foreign stocks, 32–33
  of growth and income, 171–172
  of hedge funds, 45
  of individual securities, 51–52, 67
  of money market mutual funds,
    62–63
  of municipal bonds, 38–39
  of preferred stock, 33
  of REITs, 46–47
  of zero coupon bonds, 40

Roth IRA
  deadlines and funding of, 82
  early career considerations for,
    119–120
  IRA *v.*, 78–83
  restrictions of, 78–79, 82
  rules of, 78
  taxes and, 78–83, 101–102

Saving, spending *v.*, 206–207
Screens
  for aggressive growth mutual
    funds, 195–197
  for GARP stocks, 183, 185
  for growth stocks, 181–182
  investment ideas generated from,
    160–161
  mutual funds and, 162–163
  securities and, 153
  for stocks, 173–175
  for value stocks, 183–184
Securities
  asset allocation of, 22
  growth and income with, 171–172
  screens for, 153
  taxes and, 99–100
Single security risk, 20, 27
Small cap stocks
  categorization of, 32
  large cap stocks and mid cap
    stocks *v.*, 31–32
S&P 500
  S&P Small Cap 600 and S&P
    Mid Cap 400 *v.*, 31
  various MSCI Indexes *v.*, 33
S&P Mid Cap 400, 31
S&P Small Cap 600, 31
Specialty/sector funds, 61
Spending
  priorities for, 207
  saving *v.*, 206–207

Spot, futures *v.*, 47
Standard & Poor's (S&P). *See* S&P
    500; S&P Mid Cap 400; S&P
    Small Cap 600
  bonds ratings of Moody *v.*, 38
Standard & Poor's–Goldman Sachs
    Commodities Index (S&P-GSCI),
    47–48
STARS, for equities, 161–162
Stock analysis
  of discount cash flow, 33–34
  of relative valuation, 34
  of sum-of-parts method, 34
Stocks. *See also* Common stock;
    Dividends; Equities; Foreign
    stocks; Large-cap stocks; Mid-
    cap stocks; Preferred stock;
    Small-cap stocks; Stock analysis
  analysis of value for, 33–36
  asset allocation of, 4, 10–11,
    17, 34
  asset classes and, 29
  bonds and cash *v.*, 30
  bonds *v.*, 36–37, 164–165
  conservative income with, 158–163
  growth and income with, 173–174
  individual securities and, 51–52
  inflation *v.*, 31
  international quality rankings
    for, 160
  liquidation concerns with, 33
  market liquidity of, 35
  performance factors of, 35–36
  price points for selling, 186
  purchasing, 35–36, 186
  recommendations for, 34
  risks of, 4, 30–31
  screens for, 173–175
  screens for GARP, 183, 185
  screens for growth, 181–182
  screens for value, 183–184

  shareholders rights from, 31–32
Strategic asset allocation
  advantages *v.* disadvantages, 14
  strategy of, 12, 27
Sum-of-parts method, 34

Tactical asset allocation
  advantages *v.* disadvantages, 14
  strategy of, 12–13, 27
Taxable accounts
  gains *v.* losses in, 71
  investment advice for, 70–72
  municipal bonds and, 71–72
  student loan debts and, 120
  tax-advantaged accounts *v.*,
    69–70
  taxes *v.* trades in, 70
Tax-advantaged accounts
  categories of, 72
  taxable accounts *v.*, 69–70
  TIPS and, 73
Taxes, 70. *See also* AMT; Taxable
    accounts; Tax-advantaged
    accounts
  bonds and, 164–165
  of capital gains, 98–100
  charities and, 102
  commodities and, 48
  conservative income and, 158
  corporate bonds and, 38
  Coverdell ESAs and, 87
  on dividends, 159
  employer-sponsored retirement
    plans and, 74, 101–102
  529 plans and, 86–87, 101–102
  investment accounts and, 69–70,
    98–99
  IRAs and, 77–83, 101–102
  late career concerns with, 123–124
  losses and, 101
  lowering, 99–103

middle career considerations
  with, 122
municipal bonds and, 38–39,
  101
mutual funds and, 100–101
organization for, 102
rebalancing portfolio and, 24
REITs and, 46, 72–73
Roth IRAs and, 78–83, 101–102
securities and, 99–100
zero coupon bonds and, 40
TIPS. *See* Treasury inflation
  protected securities
Treasuries
  brokers *v.*, 94–95

capital preservation and, 149–150
inflation and, 109
Treasury inflation protected
  securities (TIPS), 40–41
tax-advantaged accounts and, 73

Value
  GARP *v.*, 183
  growth *v.*, 181
  screens of stocks for, 183–184
Value at risk (VaR), 132

Wealth, 207–208, 213

Zero coupon bonds, 40